Time Out

Rome
Eating & Drinking

timeout.com/rome

Penguin Books

PENGUIN BOOKS

Published by the Penguin Group
Penguin Books Ltd, 80 Strand, London WC2R ORL, England
Penguin Books USA Inc., 375 Hudson Street, New York, New York 10014, USA
Penguin Books Australia Ltd, 250 Camberwell Road, Camberwell, Victoria 3124,
Australia
Penguin Books Canada Ltd, 10 Alcorn Avenue, Toronto, Ontario, Canada M4V 3B2
Penguin Books (NZ) Ltd, cnr Rosedale and Airborne Roads, Albany, Auckland, New
Zealand

Penguin Books Ltd, Registered Offices: Harmondsworth, Middlesex, England

First published 2002
10 9 8 7 6 5 4 3 2 1

Copyright © Time Out Group Ltd, 2002
All rights reserved

Colour reprographics by Icon, Crowne House, 56-58 Southwark Street, London
SE1 1UN
Printed and bound by Cayfosa-Quebecor, Ctra. de Caldes, Km 3 08 130 Sta,
Perpètua de Mogoda, Barcelona, Spain

Edited and designed by
Time Out Guides Limited
Universal House
251 Tottenham Court Road
London W1T 7AB
Tel + 44 (0)20 7813 3000
Fax + 44 (0)20 7813 6001
Email guides@timeout.com
www.timeout.com

Editorial
Editor Lee Marshall
Deputy Editor Christi Daugherty
Chief Reviewer Dana Klitzberg
Listings Editor Fulvia Angelini
Maps Editor Fabrizio Giusto
Proofreader Tamsin Shelton

Editorial Director Peter Fiennes
Series Editor Sarah Guy
Guides Co-ordinator Anna Norman

Design
Group Art Director John Oakey
Art Director Mandy Martin
Art Editor Scott Moore
Designers Benjamin de Lotz, Sarah Edwards,
Lucy Grant
Picture Editor Kerri Miles
Deputy Picture Editor Kit Burnet
Picture Librarian Sarah Roberts
Scanning & Imaging Dan Conway
Ad make-up Glen Impey

Advertising
Group Commercial Director Lesley Gill
Sales Director Mark Phillips
International Sales Co-ordinator Ross Canadé
Advertisement Sales (Rome)
Margherita Tedone
Advertising Assistant Sabrina Ancilleri

Administration
Chairman Tony Elliott
Managing Director Mike Hardwick
Group Financial Director Kevin Ellis
Group General Manager Nichola Coulthard
Marketing Director Christine Cort
Marketing Manager Mandy Martinez
Production Manager Mark Lamond
Production Controller Samantha Furniss
Accountant Sarah Bostock

Features in this guide were written and researched by Lee Marshall and Dana Klitzberg.

Reviews were written by Mari Beth Bittan, Sarah Delaney, Peter Douglas, John Follain, Elizabeth
Geoghegan, Phillippa Hitchen, Michelle Hough, Dana Klitzberg, Peter Loewe, Lee Marshall, Phoebe
Natanson, Alexandra Salomon, Niccolò Vivarelli, Courtney Walsh and Megan Williams.

The editor would like to thank Anne Hanley and Clara Marshall, who ate and drank beyond the call
of duty. Time Out would like to thank Ruth Jarvis.

Maps by LS International, via Sanremo 17, 20133 Milan, Italy.

Photography by Adam Eastland except page 17 AKG London.

Contents

About the guide

The reviews in this guide are based solely on the experiences of *Time Out* restaurant reviewers. All the restaurants, bars and cafés listed here were visited anonymously over a period of a few months, and *Time Out* footed the bills. No payment of any kind from restaurant owners has secured or influenced a review in this guide.

In the listings, the times given are those observed by the kitchen; in other words, the times within which one is fairly certain to be able to sit down and order a meal. These can change according to the time of year and the owners' whims. It is often a good idea to call ahead (although that's easier if you speak a little Italian). Average prices listed are per person for three courses, including service but excluding wine and other extras. For pizzerias, the price given is for one pizza and a glass of beer. Average prices have been graded on the following scale:

up to €20	€
€20 to €35	€€
€35 to €50	€€€
€50 to €80	€€€€
over €80	€€€€€

We list the credit cards accepted by the restaurant or bar by initials: AmEx (American Express), DC (Diners Club), MC (MasterCard) and V (Visa).

The star system is there to help you identify top performers at a glance. A red star ★ beside the name of a restaurant means that our reviewers found it to be one of the best in the city.

Eating
& Drinking
in Rome

In Rome, food is culture. Of course, it's unfair to set Michelangelo's frescoes in the Sistine Chapel against a plate of tonnarelli cacio e pepe, especially when the sun is shining and the wine is flowing and you've been tramping around the city all day. Suddenly there they are, the golden yellow strands, topped with a snowfall of cheese that is just beginning to melt, dusted with just enough pepper to bite.

Italian food culture has until recently been more interested in tradition than innovation and more interested in getting the ingredients right than in adding new ones. It is also a monolithic, all-encompassing beast. Whereas in London you can all but stick a pin into the globe – China, India, Russia, Thailand – to choose a restaurant, in Rome the only dilemma most of the time is whether to go for pasta or for pizza. While international restaurants do exist, and have increased in number and quality over recent years, they're still rare and exotic. Happily, though, despite the lack of Mongolian yurt-themed eateries, the Roman restaurant scene is far from static.

RIPAHOTEL
ROMA

1/3 DESIGN
1/3 WORK
1/3 PURE FUN

Take a large measure of design,
Put it in each of 170 suites.
Add one 200-seat and
one 100-seat conference room,
five break-out rooms,
the Riparte Café
and the Suite Music Club.
Stir well and
you will get the Ripa Hotel.
The perfect cocktail
for any conference. Book it.
Served daily in Trastevere,
in the heart of Rome.

ripahotel via degli orti di trastevere,1
00153 roma tel 06 58611 fax 06 5814550
www.ripahotel.com info@ripahotel.com

In the last few years, many of the traditional white-linen restaurants have been weeded out by recession and a greater demand for quality. Into the void has stepped an army of new, young establishments. Among those new young places are **Antico Arco** (*see p135*) and **Uno e Bino** (*see p201*), both of which are very hot right now.

Another recent phemomenon is the increasing number of regional cuisines represented in Rome: Neapolitan, Calabrian, Sicilian, Sardinian and marchigiano (from the Marches). Italians are so territorial that these interlopers could be numbered among the city's foreign restaurants.

The final novelty – but by no means the least significant – is the rise of the superchef in a city that has always been low on Michelin stars. While chefs in Rome traditionally were known only to nearby residents, times have changed, and the celebrity chef concept has arrived. Leader of the pack is the Italian-trained German chef Heinz Beck, who has turned **La Pergola** (*see p197*) into the place where all Roman gourmets want to eat at least once before they die. Close behind come a herd of pretenders, and at the front of the pack are Enrico Derflingher at **La Terrazza** (*see p111*) and Agata Caraccio at **Agata e Romeo** (*see p170*).

A word on nomenclature. Alongside 'ristorante' and 'pizzeria' – which should need no explanation – you are likely to come across a few other terms. A 'trattoria' is, of course, a small, family-run place, offering hearty local cuisine. An 'osteria' is, in theory, a drinking den with a limited range of basic dishes and a menu that is generally recited out loud; the same goes for the 'taverna'. But in practice, these names are increasingly fluid, and many places that describe themselves as 'osterie' are, these days, decidedly upmarket.

The menu

The canonic order of service in most restaurants is: antipasto (hors-d'oeuvres), primo (generally pasta), secondo (usually meat or fish), dessert. You are under absolutely no obligation to order a fixed number of courses, or even to respect the sequence. Ordering only two courses (primo and secondo, secondo and dessert, or even primo and dessert) is increasingly common. (For a full menu vocabulary, *see p209* **Glossary**.)

Fixed-price meals are a rarity. Top-flight establishments occasionally offer a menu degustazione (taster menu), but anywhere that displays a 'menu turistico' should generally be avoided, especially if it is written in several languages.

Drinks

Most top-range restaurants have respectable wine lists, and Italian wine has been gaining respect in recent years (for clues on cruising through the crus, *see p20*). Trattorie and osterie tend to have a limited selection: the house wine is usually an uninspiring Castelli Romani white, or an equally unimpressive Montepulciano d'Abruzzo red. There are exceptions, especially in the new breed of young, creative trattorie like **Ditirambo** (*see p89*) or **Il Dito e la Luna** (*see p200*). Note that in pizzerie, beer or Coca-Cola are the drinks of choice, though wine of some sort will always be available. Mineral water (acqua minerale) comes either frizzante/gassata (sparkling) or naturale (still). If you have a full meal, and they like you, you may be offered free amaro (bitter, herb-based liqueur) or even grappa (grape pomace brandy) to round off the proceedings.

The location
The comfort
The luxury
The taste
The attention

The detail

HOTEL DE RUSSIE

ROMA

LE JARDIN DU RUSSIE   STRAVINSKIJ BAR
DE RUSSIE SPA

Via del Babuino, 9 - 00187 Roma Italy
Tel. (39) 06 32 88 81 - Fax (39) 06 32 88 88 88
e-mail: reservations@hotelderussie.it www.roccofortehotels.com

ROCCO FORTE
HOTELS

Paying & tipping

In 1995 the city council abolished the traditional pane e coperto charge, which was basically a way of getting around low Italian tipping rates by charging diners for the privilege of having a tablecloth and a basket of stale bread. Some restaurants continue to ignore the ban, so you will likely come across it on your bill from time to time. Many others get around the ban by crossing out the word 'coperto' but leaving the word 'pane'.

Service is supposed to be included, but some places still add it as a separate charge, or make it discretionary. If in doubt, ask: 'il servizio è incluso?' Romans tend not to tip much, especially in family-run places, so waiters count on tourists for their bonuses. Basically, if you are happy with the meal, leave not less than five per cent and not more than ten per cent. Don't be ashamed to check the bill in detail: restaurateurs can become strangely innumerate when dealing with tourists.

Italy is still a cash society, so never assume you can use cards or travellers' cheques without asking first. By law, when you pay a bill (il conto) you must be given a proper receipt (una ricevuta fiscale). In theory, if you leave a restaurant without it you can incur a fine, but the chances of this happening are about the same as those of Italy winning the Six Nations rugby tournament. In practice, many of the cheapest restaurants still favour the personal approach, with the waiter sidling up and whispering the amount discreetly in your ear.

General points

Taking children into even the smartest restaurants is never a problem in Rome. This is a family culture, and Romans are extremely indulgent to children. Enthusiastic waiters will oblige with a high chair (un seggiolone), and bring mezze porzioni (half portions) on request. On the other hand, lone diners can have trouble getting a table at busy times – eating out is a communal experience here.

Booking is becoming more common, even in places that might appear to be spit and sawdust. Where booking is essential or advisable, we say as much in the body of the

review. Those coming over to Rome for a long weekend would be well advised to book any must-eats before arrival. Most Romans eat lunch between 1.30 and 2.30, and dinner anytime between 8.30 and 10pm. Restaurants rarely open for dinner before 8pm; if you want to eat before then, head for a pizzeria – most are open by 7pm.

Pizzerie

Ten years ago, you could have any pizza you liked as long as it was Roman. The city's pizzaioli have always been proud of their thinner, flatter pizza romana, but recently the fickle public has defected to the puffier Neapolitan variety. A third option has recently been provided by followers of the slow-rise method pioneered by Roman pizza guru Angelo Iezzi, though this is better adapted to takeaway outlets. It is entirely up to you which one you prefer. To learn more about the pizza controversy, *see p206.*

Whichever you choose, avoid the reheated surface-of-Mars discs that congeal outside tourist bars. Proper pizza rotonda (round pizza) should be rolled and baked – preferably in a wood oven – as you wait.

Wine bars & pubs

Neighbourhood enoteche (wine shops) and vini e oli outlets have been around in Rome since time immemorial, complete with their huddle of old men drinking wine by the glass (al bicchiere or alla mescita). More recently, a number of upmarket, international-style wine bars have sprung up, offering snacks or even full meals to go with their wines. Such is the Roman predilection for eating over drinking that some – such as **Ferrara** (*see p148*) or **Il Simposio** (*see p127*) – are better thought of as restaurants with particularly great cellars.

Bars & cafés

The neighbourhood bar still exists: the kind where Romans accompany their breakfast cappuccino with a cornetto (croissant), where lurid spirits tempt the unwary from mirrored shelves, where sawdust covers the floor and the same old white-bread tramezzini (sandwiches) and pizzette (mini-pizzas) lurk behind detergent-scented glass. Increasingly, though, the humble Roman bar is taking on new and better roles.

Vegetarian Rome

Italians have no great awareness of vegetarianism. There are Italian vegetarians, but they tend to be of the hard-line macrobiotic variety. That said, it's a lot easier for vegetarians here than in many European cities, as Italian cuisine includes innumerable meat-free combinations of pasta, cheese and vegetables.

As long as you avoid the cucina romana offal-with-everything places, you should be able to assemble a perfectly satisfying meal by choosing from among the antipasti, first courses, salads or contorni and desserts. If in doubt, check by asking 'non c'è carne, vero?' (there's no meat, is there?). Note, though, that many Italians don't consider chicken (pollo) or fish (pesce) to be meat, so always double-check.

Vegetarian-friendly first courses (primi) include orechiette ai broccoletti/cima di rape (ear-shaped pasta with broccoli sprigs/green turnip-tops), pasta e ceci (soup with pasta and chick-peas), pasta e fagioli (soup with pasta and borlotti beans), pasta alla puttanesca or alla checca (literally 'à la whore' or 'à la queen' – based on olives, capers and tomatoes, though anchovies (alici) are sometimes slipped in), penne all'arrabbiata (pasta with tomato sauce and lots of chilli), and ravioli ricotta e spinaci (cottage cheese and spinach), served 'con burro e salvia' (with butter and sage) or with a simple sugo di pomodoro (tomato sauce).

Second courses are more of a problem. Often, you'll have to make do with an uninspiring insalata mista. Among the standard options are the carciofi alla giudia (deep-fried artichokes), fagioli all'uccelletto (haricot beans with tomato, garlic and olive oil – strictly speaking a contorno, but substantial enough to take the place of a main course) – and melanzane alla parmigiana (aubergine with parmesan – note that this occasionally has meat in the topping).

Some of the best vegetarian restaurants in town are listed in the guide, including the two top choices for local veggies **Arancia Blu** (*see p200*); **Margutta Vegetariano Ristorante** (*see p38*).

In tourist hotspots, such as piazza Navona or piazza del Pantheon, most bars double up as restaurant, pizzeria and gelateria. Almost all share the two characteristics of the safe, multilingual tourist haven: mediocre food and extortionate prices. As long as you don't think you're getting a taste of the real Rome, they can be wonderful places for a rest and a look at life in the square. More positively, in areas with large daytime office populations (often just around the corner from the tourist traps), bars have taken over much of the territory of the trattoria, as the Italian lunchbreak comes into line with the one-hour EU average. Many offer a good range of rolls and salads, often backed up by one or two hot dishes. These can be a great place for a cheap, filling and often surprisingly good lunch.

There is little difference between il bar and il caffè, except that the latter tends to be more daytime and coffee-oriented. The same rules apply to both: non-regulars are expected to pay at the cassa (cash register) before consuming, so you should identify what you want before you pay. Put the scontrino (receipt) down on the bar counter when ordering; placing a coin on top of it can

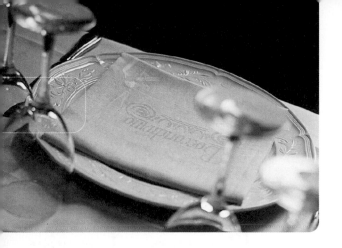

help to attract the bartender's attention. If you choose to sit down, you will be served by a waiter and charged at least double for the privilege.

Along with snacks, bars generally offer spremute (freshly squeezed juice – generally orange or grapefruit). A few also have frullati (fruit shakes) and centrifughe (blended juices, especially of carrot or apple). Water from the tap is free; a glass of mineral water (acqua minerale) costs €0.30-€0.60. Caffè freddo (iced coffee) and sugary tè freddo (iced tea) are part of the standard bill of fare in summer.

Reading the reviews

Average prices listed in this guide are per person for three courses (generally primo, secondo and dessert), including service but excluding wine and other extras. For pizzerie, the price given is for one pizza, one extra (such as a bruschetta) and a glass of beer.

The times given are those observed by the kitchen; in other words, the times within which one is fairly sure of being able to sit down and order a meal. These can change according to the time of year and the owners' whims.

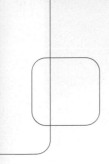

The **cuisine**
of Rome & Lazio

Despite its firm place on the world's most-visited list, the Eternal City is not known as a culinary mecca. Though smaller, Florence, Bologna and Genoa all have more distinctive gastronomic traditions. This has something to do with Rome's lack of an obvious signature dish. But it is also in the nature of a tradition that is not unified, but made up of several strands: the Roman Jewish tradition, the local taste for slaughterhouse offcuts and, finally, the influence of the huge influx of immigrants from Lazio.

All of these strands are rooted in cucina povera – the cooking of the common people. The city specialises in the sort of hearty fare exemplified by one of the most reproduced genre paintings of the Italian baroque, Annibale Carracci's *The Bean-Eater* (pictured). Accordingly, Rome has become the trattoria capital of the world, chock-full of neighbourhood eateries that serve different takes on the handful of Roman dishes that appear on every menu.

Like their cousins further south, Romans are heavy consumers of pasta. Bucatini all'amatriciana is perhaps the best example of the local less-is-more equation:

aromatic onions, smoky, pungent guanciale (cured pork cheek) and ripe tomatoes sautéd with olive oil and tossed with pasta. Other pasta dishes for which Rome is noted are spaghetti alla carbonara (with a bacon, egg and parmesan sauce) and tonnarelli cacio e pepe (thin flat strands served with grated hard goat's cheese and lots of black pepper).

The city's proximity to the Tyrrhenian coast means that seafood is readily available, but only recently has 'luxury' white fish like spigola (sea bass), orata (sea bream) and rombo (turbot) found a place on the Roman table (served roasted with potatoes, or baked whole in a crust of sea salt that permeates the skin and flavours the delicate white flesh). The local tradition of cucina povera tended to ignore the finny tribe, with two exceptions: salt cod and sting ray. The former, known as baccalà, is still imported from Norway in rock-hard slabs, which are then softened in running water and served stewed in a tomato sauce; you can see soaking cod in most alimentari (grocers) on Fridays, the canonical day for the dish. Arzilla (sting ray) goes into the classic minestra al brodo

di arzilla. Today, bivalves and crustaceans also form part of the local diet, expecially cozze (mussels) and vongole (clams). In general, though, Rome is carnivore heaven. The celebrated abbacchio a scottadito (baby lamb chops) is a savoury speciality. Romans are equally proud of their saltimbocca – thinly pounded veal escalopes topped with ham and sage leaves, sautéd in a pan with a touch of white wine. The basic pollo alla romana is chicken stewed with tomatoes, peppers, and onions – a good winter warmer.

The city's neighbourhood markets are a cornucopia of fresh, colourful vegetables. One of the most Roman of vegetables is the artichoke, used in dishes like carciofi alla romana (cooked until meltingly tender with garlic, parsley, wild mint and pecorino cheese) and carciofi alla giudia (twice-fried). Another speciality is puntarelle (chicory stems sliced thinly and served as a salad, and tossed in a tangy anchovy dressing).

Of course, Italy would not be Italy without those sweet, sun-warmed, green-to-red salad tomatoes. Tucking into a caprese salad of ripe tomatoes, olive oil, fresh buffalo milk mozzarella and basil while sitting in a sunny piazza is one of the great pleasures of Italian dining.

On the market

Rome's produce markets are part of the living, breathing fabric of the city. Even if you're not planning to take a kilo of red peppers home with you, they're worth a visit for their sheer beauty.

The most celebrated and photogenic is the bustling, colourful food and flower market of Campo de' Fiori. Fruit and vegetables are the main act, but there are also fish stalls and, in the autumn, a mushroom man offering baskets of plump funghi porcini and delicate orange-brown gallinelle. Equally picturesque are the tiny clusters of stalls in piazza delle Coppelle, near the Pantheon, and in via delle Scuderie, just along the road from the Trevi Fountain.

But these are definitely not the cheapest markets in the city. For real bargains, head for piazza Vittorio, Rome's main retail produce market, which is still referred to thus, even though it no longer stands in piazza Vittorio. After years of municipal shilly-shallying, it was recently moved to via Guglielmo Pepe, down the southern side of Termini train station. With large North African and Asian communities in the area, the usual fresh produce, cheese and meat are supplemented by pulses, halal meat and spices.

In Trastevere, the bustling market in piazza San Cosimato retains some of its traditional neighbourhood feel, and has fair prices. One of the best and cheapest markets in the centre, though, is the serious, maze-like covered market in piazza Testaccio, which features among its other attractions the fish stall of the Mastroianni brothers, cousins of the great Marcello (and to prove it they keep a group photo hanging above the sole and anchovies).

Food markets in Rome tend to open from 6am to 2pm, Monday to Saturday.

The rise
& rise of
Italian wine

Italian wine has taken a great leap forward in the last ten years. Not that you would know it unless you've spent some time in the bel paese: for one of the paradoxes of the Italian wine revolution is that only the faintest echoes of its achievements reach foreign markets. British supermarkets and bottle shops continue to stock the same old Chiantis, Lambruscos and Soaves, many of them bottled especially for export under labels that even the best-informed Italian wine connoisseur would never recognise.

The specialist importers in Britain and the States have begun to sit up and take note, but, even today, the only real way to take stock of the quality and variety of modern Italian wine is to get on a plane and come to Italy.

This is a land where the small producer is king. Wine is grown in every Italian region, often by farmers who tend a small plot of vines among their other crops: the average vineyard takes up less than one hectare. Even quality wineries are often relatively small family concerns, producing fewer than 10,000 bottles a year. This is one of the reasons why the export market is such a poor reflection of the state of play. In Australia, for example, four companies account for 80 per cent of the annual crush, and their financial muscle is an important factor in the international success of Australian wines. The situation in California is similar. In Italy, on the other hand, the big wineries – Antinori, Frescobaldi, Duca di Salaparuta (the

Corvo people), Fontana Candida – are still small fish compared to the Southcorps or Gallos of this world. For the wine buff, though, this fragmentation has important advantages. It means that there are always new discoveries to be made. It means that there has been no corporate-fuelled Chardonnay and Cabernet Sauvignon invasion.

Of Italy's 20 most commonly planted grapes, only one (merlot) is not native to the country. Sangiovese and nebbiolo are the best-known native grapes: the first provides the backbone of Chianti Classico and Brunello di Montalcino, the second underpins the great Piedmontese red, Barolo. But there are other, smaller varieties that are capable of greatness, like greco in Campania, aglianico in Campania and Basilicata and nero d'avola in Sicily.

The dominance of small wineries also means that vineyard visits are not channelled through smoothly run visitors' centres as they are in the Napa or Hunter Valleys. Instead – providing you ring ahead – the wine producers are usually there to open bottles, answer questions and lead a tour of their vines and cellars.

The other eminently Italian phenomenon is the cantine sociali – co-operative cellars that buy the grapes of hundreds of stakeholder farmers and turn them into wine. Until recently, they were synonymous with low-grade plonk, but now some of the cantine sociali, especially in the north, have begun to outclass many private domaines. A case in point is the Cantina Produttori San Michele Appiano, from Italy's partially German-speaking Alto Adige region. Under the direction of kellermeister Hans Terzer, this humble

Campania Ischia

cellar has become one of the top Italian producers of fragrant white wines. If you see a bottle of its Sauvignon St Valentin, or its cousin, Sauvignon Lahn, grab it.

Italian wine regulations are labyrinthine and shackled by bureaucracy, though recent changes have made them a little more flexible and responsive to the market. However, many producers still prefer to sidestep the problem of outdated criteria by bottling their more audacious creations as plain old 'vino da tavola'. These 'super-vini-da-tavola', like Tignanello or Vintage Tunina, are often more expensive and more prestigious than better-known wines – a typically Italian paradox.

Per capita wine consumption fell in Italy by more than 50 per cent between 1960 and 1990. This is another Italian wine paradox: though it is the world's second-largest producer of wine, close behind France, Italy has somehow bred a generation of young people who prefer to drink beer, Coca-Cola or mineral water with their fettuccine. However, the slow demise of wine – any old wine, the rougher the better – as the natural accompaniment to the family meal is balanced by a growing appreciation of quality wine.

In 1990 you could count the number of by-the-glass wine bars in Rome on the fingers of one hand, now there are dozens. Some, like the funky backroom space of the gastronomic shop **'Gusto** (*see p36*), are clearly inspired by shops in London and New York, and favour the description 'wine bar' in English. Others, like **Angolo Divino** (*see p100*), have that born-again antique bottle-shop look, and prefer the label enoteca or even vini e oli – 'wine and oil emporium'. Still others, like **Ferrara** (*see p148*) or **Il Simposio** (*see p127*), have blurred the line between wine bars and restaurants, bringing them close to a gaggle of new restaurants that take wine very seriously, like **Uno e Bino** (*see p201*) or **Al Bric** (*see p82*) and **Al Ciabot** (*see p83*).

All in all, it's never been a better time for Italian wine, and there's never been a better place to drink it than Rome. Unlike Florence or Venice, which tend to push their own regional wines, Rome tends to be more ecumenical; a typical wine bar's mescita (by the glass) selection is likely to include wines from Tuscany, Piedmont, Sicily and Campania. Not to mention Lazio, the local region.

Gelato

Ice-cream as we know it today was born in Italy in the 17th century. That is about as much as we can assert without treading on national pride (the French refuse to give up the sorbet, at the very least, without a fight) or straying into culinary mythology. Far less controversial is the fact that, despite transatlantic imitators, Italy is still home to the best gelato in the world.

Rome is as good a place as anywhere to go on an ice-cream binge. Still, although even the lurid, semi-industrial products passed off as gelato artigianale (home-made ice-cream) by many neighbourhood bars beat Mr Whippy hands down, it still pays to be selective. While most Roman ice-cream is OK, some of it is excellent. But you have to be prepared to put in a bit of legwork: with a few exceptions, many of the best places are out in the sticks.

Any self-respecting gelateria will have at least 20 flavours. Real gelato heads separate the sheep from the goats by sticking to the two benchmark flavours: chocolate (cioccolato) and hazelnut (nocciola). Both are surprisingly difficult to do well. To bring out the flavour, it helps to use the best ingredients. This doctrine was taken to an extreme by the iconoclastic brothers who founded **Il Gelato di San Crispino** (*see opposite*) in the early 1990s – to the extent that only 20-year-old barrel-aged Marsala from a Sicilian winery goes into their trademark zabaione. But even the traditionalists, who add hand-made flavours created from fresh fruits, juices and sauces to a prepared base, can still get the formula so right that the raspberry flavoured ice-cream tastes more real than the real thing.

In summer, it's also worth seeking out and sampling a grattachecca. This is a noble and time-honoured Roman version of water-ice, in which hand-grated ice is scooped into a cup and covered in sweet, sticky fruit syrup or juice. Once Rome was full of kiosks selling this treat; but these days ice-cream has usurped it, and now only a handful are left, including the Trastevere institution listed here.

Gelateria

Alberto Pica
*Via della Seggiola 12 (06
686 8405). Bus/tram to via
Arenula.* **Open** *Nov-Mar* 8am-
1am Mon-Sat. *Apr-Oct* 8am-
2am Mon-Sat; 4pm-3am
Sun. Closed 2wks Aug.
No credit cards.
A small but excellent selection
of flavours, among which the
rice specialities stand out:
imagine eating frozen, partially
cooked rice pudding, and
you're getting warm. The
riso alla cannella (cinnamon
rice) is particularly delicious.

Il Gelato di San Crispino
*Via della Panetteria 42
(06 679 3924). Metro
Barberini/bus to via del
Tritone.* **Open** noon-12.30am
Mon-Thur, Sun; noon-1.30am
Fri, Sat. Closed mid Jan-mid
Feb. **No credit cards**.
Currently the best ice-cream in
Rome. The secret is an
obsessive control over the
whole process. Some flavours
(zabaione – made with 20-year-
old barrel-aged Marsala –
meringa al cioccolato,
pistacchio) are fixtures,
while others change by season.
In summer, the lampone
(raspberry) and susine (yellow
plum) are fabulous; in winter
arancia selvatica (wild orange).
Branch via Acaia 56
(06 7045 0412).

Sora Mirella
*Lungotevere degli Anguillara,
by ponte Cestio (no phone).
Bus to ponte Cestio.* **Open**
May-Sept 10am-3am daily.
Mirella styles herself 'la regina
della grattachecca' (the queen
of water ices), and there
seems no reason to disagree.
True to tradition, ice is grated
by hand here with an iron
glove. Sit on the Tiber wall as
you tuck into the speciale
superfrutta – fresh melon,
kiwi fruit and strawberry,
or whatever's in season.

Café du Parc
*Piazza di Porta San Paolo (06
574 3363). Metro Piramide.*
Open *Oct-Apr* 5am-9pm Mon-
Thur, Sun; 5am-1am Fri, Sat.
May-Sept 4.30am-2am daily.
No credit cards.
The gelati in this kiosk bar
near Piramide are excellent,
especially the cremolati, which
is a kind of creamy sorbet.
If it's available, try the
astonishingly good raspberry.
The coffee and stracciatella
also stand out here, however
table service can be offhand,
and doesn't come cheap.

Giolitti
*Via Vespucci 35 (06 574
6006). Bus/tram to via
Marmorata.* **Open** 7am-
midnight Mon, Tue,
Thur-Sun. Closed 2wks
Aug. **No credit cards**.

▶

No, not the famous Giolitti in the centre, which is one of Rome's most overrated gelaterie. This Giolitti is a rather shabby bar just off via Marmorata, with an excellent range of classic gusti and an outstanding zabaione. There is also good granita di caffè – a coffee-ice drink.

Monti, Esquilino & San Giovanni

Il Palazzo del Freddo di Giovanni Fassi
Via Principe Eugenio 65-7 (06 446 4740). Metro Vittorio. **Open** noon-midnight Tue-Fri; noon-1am Sat; 10am-midnight Sun. **No credit cards**.
With its pompous name, breathtakingly kitsch interior and splendid ices, Fassi is a Roman institution. Its walls are adorned with Edwardian adverts and Fascist-era posters extolling the virtues of the shop's wares. Service is irascible, but the ices are sublime. Best of all the gusti are riso (rice pudding) and the Palazzo's own invention, la caterinetta, which is a divine and mysterious concoction involving much whipped honey and creamy vanilla.

North

Duse
Via Eleonora Duse 1E (06 807 9300). Bus or tram to piazza Ungheria. **Open** 8am-midnight Mon-Sat. Closed 1wk Aug. **No credit cards**.

In this otherwise entirely residential neighbourhood, Duse attracts well-off parioline (local rich kids) on their motorbikes in search of excitement. Late at night, the scene outside looks like a well-brushed street party. Try the cioccolato fondente (dark chocolate) or cioccolato bianco (white chocolate).

San Filippo
Via di Villa San Filippo 2/10 (06 807 9314). Bus or tram to piazza Ungheria. **Open** Nov-Mar 7am-10pm Tue-Thur; 7am-midnight Fri-Sun. *May-Oct* 7am-midnight Tue-Sun. **No credit cards**.
Just around the corner from Duse, this apparently modest bar/latteria is a serious challenger. Sample the nocciola (hazelnut) and cioccolato; or try one from the big range of seasonal fruits, including anguria (watermelon).

South

Petrini dal 1926
Piazza dell'Alberone 16A (06 786 307). Metro Furio Camillo/bus to via Appia Nuova. **Open** 10.30am-1am Tue-Sun. Closed Dec, Jan. **No credit cards**.
As its name implies, this gelateria on the Appia Nuova has been purveying ice-cream for decades, and many still consider its products – based on meticulously sourced ingredients – to be the best in Rome. The zabaione and nocciola are particularly worthy.

Where to...

DO BRUNCH

Tridente
Babington's (daily)
Ciampini al Café du Jardin (daily)
Il Leoncino (Sun)

Navona
Bar del Fico (Sun)
Bloom (Sat, Sun)
Le Cornacchie (Sun)
Trinity College (Sun)
Margutta Vegetariano
Ristorante (Sun)

Fiori & Ghetto
Le Bain (Sat, Sun)
Wine Time (Sun)

Trastevere & Monteverde
Stardust (Sun)

Monti, Termini & S Giovanni
La Gallina Bianca (Sat)

GET SERIOUS COFFEE

Tridente
Rosati
Vitti

Navona
La Caffettiera
Sant'Eustacchio
Tazza d'Oro

Trevi & Veneto
Caffè Traforo

Vatican, Prati & West
Faggiani

Monti, Termini & S Giovanni
Antico Caffè del Brasile

Suburbs
Il Cigno

TAKE THE PARENTS

Tridente
Edy
Gino in vicolo Rosini
Nino

Navona
Alfredo e Ada

Fiori & Ghetto
Costanza
Da Giggetto
Piperno
Vecchia Roma

Trevi & Veneto
Al Presidente
Sans Souci
Tullio

Trastevere & Monteverde
Alberto Ciarla
Checco er Carrettiere

Suburbs
Al Ceppo
Cecilia Metella

TAKE THE KIDS

Fiori & Ghetto
Acchiappafantasmi

Vatican, Prati & West
Zen

Trastevere & Monteverde
Il Boom
Da Ivo
Dar Poeta

Aventine & Testaccio
La Torricella

Suburbs
Al Forno della Soffitta
Gaudì
Itoyo

TAKE A DATE

Navona
Il Convivio
Myosotis
Osteria dell'Ingegno

Trevi & Veneto
Al Presidente

Trastevere & Monteverde
Antico Arco

Monti, Termini & S Giovanni
Agata e Romeo

Suburbs
Al Ponte della Ranocchia
Uno e Bino

SEE AND BE SEEN

Tridente
Ciro
Fiaschetteria Beltramme

Navona
Bar del Fico
Bar della Pace
Bloom
Il Cantuccio
Maccheroni
Santa Lucia

Fiori & Ghetto
Le Bain
Sciam

Trastevere & Monteverde
Riparte Café
Stardust

Aventine & Testaccio
Ketumbar

Suburbs
Duke's
La Pergola dell'Hotel Hilton

ENJOY THE VIEW

Tridente
Ciampini al Café du Jardin

Trevi & Veneto
La Terrazza dell'Hotel Eden

Suburbs
La Pergola dell'Hotel Hilton

DINE AL FRESCO

Tridente
Dal Bolognese

Navona
Il Bacaro
Osteria dell'Antiquario

Fiori & Ghetto
Ar Galletto
Camponeschi
Il Gonfalone
La Carbonara
La Taverna degli Amici

Trastevere & Monteverde
Augusto
Panattoni

Aventine & Testaccio
Al Callarello
La Torricella
San Teodoro

Suburbs
Caffè delle Arti
Cecilia Metella

DINE WITH HISTORY

Fiori & Ghetto
Costanza
Da Vezio
Il Goccetto
Il Gonfalone

Aventine & Testaccio
Checchino dal 1887

Tridente

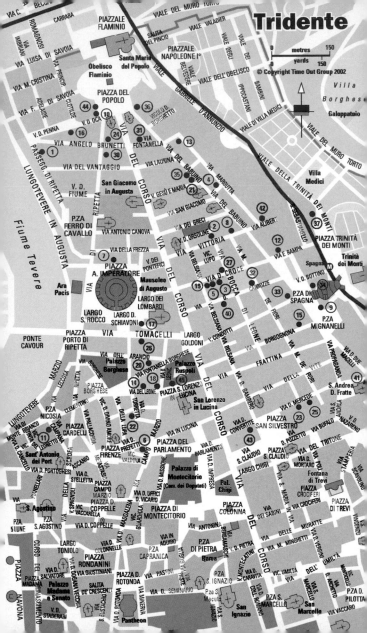

The three-pronged trident of streets south of piazza del Popolo was once part of the Campus Martius, ancient Rome's military training ground. In the 18th and 19th centuries the area around the Spanish Steps became the centre of Rome's foreign community – especially its more bohemian, artistic fringe. Today, this is Rome's fashion triangle, with the designer boutiques clustering around the parallel streets of via dei Condotti and via Borgognona. As one might expect, the dining options in this area tend to be fairly upmarket. With its historic bars and cafés, this is also one of the best areas in Rome to go on an aperitivo crawl.

Restaurants

Antico Bottaro

Passeggiata di Ripetta 15 (06 323 6763). Metro Flaminio/bus to via Ripetta. **Meals served** 8pm-midnight Tue-Sun. Closed 2-3wks Aug. **Average** €€€-€€€€. **Credit** AmEx, DC, MC, V.

This civilised, late-opening restaurant near piazza del Popolo does seafood with a southern Italian slant. Housed in a warren of pale yellow rooms with vaulted ceilings, it offers a good fusion of tradition with modernity, though its refined elegance comes at a price. Main courses include an excellent insalata di polipo con salsa agli agrumi (octopus salad in citrus sauce), while an unlikely sounding tagliolini di pesce spada affumicato al curry e pinoli (pasta with curried smoked swordfish and pine nuts) is a surprisingly successful combination. Service is courteous, and there is a broad selection of Italian wines.

Ciro ★

Via Vittoria 22 (06 361 4148). Metro Spagna/bus to via del Babuino. **Meals served** 8-11pm Mon-Sat. Closed Aug. **Average** €€€€€. **Credit** AmEx, DC, MC, V.

Just down the road from the Spanish Steps, the place is full of television personalities, minor celebrities and models air-kissing a path to their tables. The seaside decor borders on the kitsch: elaborate coral and shell light fixtures deck the walls. The waiters are so solicitous that you wish they would ignore you for a while; and the

Gino in vicolo Rosini. *See p36.*

prices are fierce. But the food makes up for such minor annoyances: the antipasto di pesce crudo (raw fish starter) is out of this world. Pasta dishes like tagliatelle with lobster and spaghetti alle vongole (with baby clams) are delicious and abundant. Save room for the light, creamy mille foglie (millefeuille) dessert.

Dal Bolognese

Piazza del Popolo 1/2 (06 361 1426). Metro Flaminio/bus to piazza del Popolo. **Meals served** 8.15-11.15pm Tue; 12.45-3pm, 8.15-11.15pm Wed-Sun. **Average** €€€€. **Credit** AmEx, DC, MC, V.

This Roman institution on the marvellously scenographic piazza del Popolo is a must. Not, though, for the basic but high-quality food, which includes delicious hand-cut San Daniele ham (prosciutto di San Daniele), pappardelle (wide fettuccine) with duck ragu, grilled seafood plate and a celebrated bollito misto (a tray of mixed boiled meats served with a green sauce – a Bolognese speciality). The

real reason to drop in on Dal Bolognese – above and beyond the ultra-professional service and the ample wine list – is the scene, daahling, the scene. All around are film producer types smoking cigars and women who are just a little too thin and a little too all-over-tanned – and they all seem to know each other.

Di fronte a

Via della Croce 37 (06 678 0355). Metro Spagna/bus to via del Corso. **Meals served** 11am-midnight Tue-Sun. Closed 10 days Jan. **Average** €-€€. **Credit** AmEx, DC, MC, V.

This is something of a hybrid: a place where you can grab a quick coffee, lounge over a cocktail or sit down in front of a pizza or a plate of pasta. The policy of Di fronte a ('across the road from') is to spread itself thinly, offering punters a bit of everything, even when other eateries are in the grip of the afternoon siesta. While the cuisine may not be exactly haute and the decor not as striking as when the place opened in the late '90s, the sheer range of the menu is admirable. Vegetarians have a particularly good deal with a whole array of house insalatone (giant salads) and such calorific delights as the gran fritto vegetariano (deep-fried courgette flowers, olives, sliced apple and buffalo mozzarella) from which to choose.

Edy

Vicolo del Babuino 4 (06 3600 1738). Metro Spagna/bus to via del Babuino. **Meals served** 12.15-3.30pm, 6.30pm-midnight Mon-Sat. Closed Aug. **Average** €€. **Credit** AmEx, DC, MC, V.

A vaguely arty trattoria crammed with second-rate canvases, which does creative but genuine Roman fish and meat cooking at reasonable prices: not bad in an area where the whiff of serious money is all-pervasive. The menu changes with the season, though the house speciality – spaghetti al cartoccio con frutti di mare, a spaghetti and seafood creation baked and served in its own silver-foil packet – is always available.

Fiaschetteria Beltramme

Via della Croce 39 (no phone). Metro Spagna/bus to via Tomacelli. **Meals served** noon-3pm, 8-11pm Mon-Sat. Closed 2wks Aug. **Average** €€. **No credit cards**.

Don't be fooled by the 'no phone, no credit cards' line and the dowdy bohemian decor. Also known as 'Da Cesaretto' after the ever-present owner, this historic trattoria is so trendy that Madonna once fled a gala dinner to eat here. Specialities include tonnarelli cacio e pepe (with sheep's cheese and pepper) and straccetti con rucola (beef strips with rocket), to be washed down with a flask of the drinkable house wine. No bookings are taken, so unless you're Madonna you'll have to join the queue outside.

You may not have come to Rome to buy meat, but at least take a look in the window of Annibale Mastroddi (via Ripetta 236/7), a jewel of a butcher's shop.

Gino in vicolo Rosini ★

*Vicolo Rosini 4 (06 687 3434). Bus to piazza San
Silvestro.* **Meals served** 1-2.45pm, 8-10.30pm Mon-Sat.
Closed Aug. **Average** €€. **No credit cards**.
In a lane around the back of the main parliament building,
and usually filled with politicians, political journalists and
hangers-on, this unreconstructed osteria is a monument
unto itself. The cuisine champions the lighter Roman
tradition in dishes like coniglio al vino bianco (rabbit in
white wine) and zucchine ripiene (stuffed courgettes);
desserts include own-made crostate (jam tarts) and an
excellent tiramisù. Come early, especially at lunchtime, or
be prepared to wait for one of the hotly contested tables.

'Gusto

*Piazza Augusto Imperatore 9 (06 322 6273/www.gusto.it).
Bus to piazza Augusto Imperatore.* **Open** *Restaurant*
1-3pm, 8pm-midnight daily. *Pizzeria* 12.30-3pm, 7.30pm-
1am daily. *Wine bar* 11am-2am daily. **Average** €€-€€€.
Credit AmEx, MC, V.
One of the most talked-about 1990s dining novelties in
Rome, 'Gusto is a multi-purpose complex with a pizzeria,
restaurant, wine bar, cook's shop and bookshop. The
ground floor pizza bar is almost always packed, and it
pays to book if you want to try its reasonably priced
pizzas and abundant salads. The upstairs restaurant
looks like a Pottery Barn advert. The menu here has a
fusion slant, and on paper it's refreshing (for Rome) to see
ingredients such as lemongrass, poppy seeds and ginger.
But the ambitious dishes – like an appetizer of tartare di
tonno e manzo con condimenti mediterranei e orientali
(tuna and beef tartar with Mediterranean and oriental
condiments) – don't always work on the plate. Pudding
can make up for it, though. The tortino al cioccolato
piccante is a dome of dense chocolate mousse with a
hidden centre of truffles spiked with hot peppers.

La Campana

*Vicolo della Campana 18 (06 6867 820). Bus to
lungotevere Marzio or via Tomacelli.* **Meals served**
12.30-3.15pm, 7.30-11.30pm Tue-Sun. Closed Aug.
Average €€€. **Credit** AmEx, DC, MC, V.
Some things never change. La Campana, which claims to
be the oldest trattoria in Rome, is one of those. The waiters
don't quite go back to 1518 – the year the place supposedly
opened its doors – but they do seem to have stepped out
of the 1950s. The clientele of journalists, politicos and
Guccis appears equally unfazed by social and culinary
revolutions. The kitchen does conservative renditions of
Roman classics – ossobuco, abbacchio and spaghetti con
le vongole. In spring, don't miss the vignarola – a once-
common broad bean, pea and ham soup.

'Gusto

Mangiamoci

Via di San Sebastianello (06 678 0546). Metro Spagna.
Average €€€. Meals served 7pm-midnight Tue-Sun.
Closed 1wk Aug. **Credit** AmEx, DC, MC, V.
Mangiamoci ('Let's eat each other') is the type of
restaurant that appeals to the under-30 Roman wannabe-
jet set. The determinedly high-tech look is more New
York than Roman, with low lighting and exposed
industrial air chutes offset by yellow- and orange-
splashed chairs. A cocktail bar out front mixes long
drinks and light aperitifs. The menu is less adventurous
than the decor, offering standard antipasti, own-made
pasta and a wide array of second courses including
ostrich steaks and duck. The maltagliati pasta with basil,
squid and potato was reasonably tasty, as was the
caciottina taglierini – linguine-style pasta served in a
hollowed caciotta cheese.

Margutta Vegetariano Ristorante ★

Via Margutta 118 (06 3265 0577). Metro Flaminio/bus to piazza del Popolo. **Meals served** 12.30-3.30pm, 7.30-11pm daily. **Average** €€. **Credit** DC, MC, V.

Rome's historic vegetarian diner occupies a large plant-filled space on arty, exclusive via Margutta. The decor pays homage to the area, with plenty of modern art. At lunch (Mon-Sat), a set-price one-plate buffet (€10, with water and dessert) is an alternative to the more formal restaurant, which offers a meatless slant on modern Italian cuisine, with one or two oriental touches. On Sunday, the fixed lunch menu is replaced by a filling all-you-can-eat €23 brunch.

Matricianella ★

Via del Leone 3/4 (06 683 2100). Bus to lungotevere Marzio. **Meals served** 12.30-3pm, 7.30-11pm Mon-Sat. Closed Aug. **Average** €€. **Credit** AmEx, DC, MC, V.

This is a good example of how to successfully upgrade the Roman family trattoria without betraying its roots. Spread over three cosy rooms, Matricianella is a friendly, bustling place with efficient, unpretentious service and great prices. The Roman imprint is most evident in classics such as bucatini all'amatriciana (pasta with a sauce of tomato, chilli, onions and sausage) but there are many more creative options, including a tasty risotto mantecato con fiori di zucca (creamy risotto with courgette flowers) and some great fritti (fried dishes) like bucce di patate – potato peel. The well-chosen wine list is a model of honest pricing. Once you've eaten here, you'll understand why it's almost always packed – so make sure you book ahead.

Nino

Via Borgognona 11 (06 679 5676). Metro Spagna. **Meals served** 12.30-3pm, 7.30-11pm Mon-Sat. Closed Aug. **Average** €€€. **Credit** AmEx, DC, MC, V.

At the Spanish Steps end of Rome's most exclusive fashion street, Nino opened its doors for business in 1934. Little except the prices seem to have changed since then. With its wood-panelled walls, old prints and mirrors, this is a safe bet for a reliable meal in the company of local businessmen, fashion folk and well-heeled tourists. The Tuscan slant comes through in dishes like ribollita (a minestrone with black cabbage and bread) and grilled Florentine steak, but the menu extends to cover most of Italy. Over the years the chefs have become so used to dealing with wafer-thin supermodels that there are even a few vegetarian options. But the fritti misti (assorted meat and veg fry-ups) are much more representative of the house mission to provide decent, high-class comfort food for the nannied rich.

Upmarket grocer Delucchi (via della Croce 75) harks back to the days when pineapples were strictly for toffs. Come here to stock up on *pistacchi* and crystallised fruit.

Penna d'Oca

Via della Penna 53 (06 3202 898). Metro Flaminio/bus to piazza del Popolo. **Meals served** 8pm-12.30am Mon-Sat. Closed 3wks Aug. **Average** €€€-€€€€. **Credit** AmEx, DC, MC, V.

A 1980s-style entrance gives on to a low dining space with white brick walls, white-painted beams and lots of chintzy detail. It doesn't quite hang together; and the same goes for the ambitious pan-Italian creations of chef Cristian Ferretti. With over 50 separate items, the menu is too all-encompassing, and dishes like fusilli caserecci al pesto di olive, pinoli, prezzemolo e pecorino (pesto of olives, pine nuts, parsley and pecorino cheese), or scorfano con pomodorini pachino in salsa di broccoletti siciliani (scorpion fish with cherry tomatoes in a broccoli sauce) smack too much of the international hotel restaurant. But the speciality risotto primi and soufflè desserts are well done, and the service is professional.

Reef. *See p40.*

Reef

*Piazza Augusto Imperatore 42 (06 6830 1430). Bus to
via Tomacelli.* **Meals served** 8-11.30pm Mon, Tue;
1-3pm, 8-11.30pm Wed-Sun. Closed 3wks Aug.
Average €€€. **Credit** AmEx, DC, MC, V.

With its cracked-glass walls, blond wood and soaring
ceilings, Reef is a hip, sleek novelty – more London than
Rome. Often this means that a place will be out of fashion
before you can say 'swordfish carpaccio'; but Reef has
been going strong for a couple of years. The raw seafood
antipasto for two is fresh, if bland; but the zuppa di ceci,
polpo, e rosmarino (puréed chickpea soup with octopus
and rosemary) sings with flavour and velvety texture.
Main courses run the gamut from sushi and sashimi to
unusual Italian-based seafood preparations. The desserts
offer a twist on molten chocolate cake, here served with
Banyuls-poached pear and rice pudding gelato.

Settimio all'Arancio

Via dell'Arancio 50 (06 687 6119). Bus to via Tomacelli.
Average €€. **Meals served** 12.30-3.30pm, 7.30-11.30pm
Mon-Sat. **Credit** AmEx, DC, MC, V.

In three rooms with functional trattoria decor, this
bustling Centro Storico food factory processes crowds of
local office workers and passing tourists. The vast menu
is pan-Italian, with the occasional more Roman dish, such
as abbacchio al forno con le patate (oven-baked lamb with
potatoes). Primi such as spaghetti cozze, vongole e
rughetta (with mussels, clams and rocket) are unrefined
but appetizing; even the dodgy-sounding farafalle al
curry is surprisingly good. The chef has obviously done
a course in dessert presentation, as a perfectly ordinary
tiramisù came dressed up to the nines. The waiters, with
their stripy waistcoats, are fast and efficient, and wine is
on offer at a very reasonable mark-up.

Tad Café

Via del Babuino 155A (06 3269 5123). Metro Spagna.
Meals served *Bar* 10.30am-8pm daily. *Restaurant* noon-
3.30pm daily. **Average** €€€. **Credit** AmEx, DC, MC, V.

This overpriced daytime café-restaurant for label lovers
is a resolute answer to those who accuse the Roman
eating scene of being all substance and no style. A narrow
outside courtyard with rafters from which blob lights
hang like high tech pears provides an alternative to the
minimalist main room. The menu, overseen by superchef
Antony Genovese, does a terrific job at mixing creative
Italian (zuppa di lenticchie e salsice al finocchietto – lentil
and sausage soup with wild fennel) with Eastern
influences (noodles di riso con manzo e salsa di fagioli
neri – rice noodles with beef and black bean sauce). On
Sundays, a more laid-back American-style brunch is

served. The food does not always live up to its ambitions, but if you want to get as close to Milan as you can without leaving Rome, this is the place. There are plans to begin serving dinner here.

Vic's ★
Vicolo della Torretta 60 (06 687 1445). Bus to piazza San Silvestro. **Meals served** 12.30-3pm, 7.30-11pm Mon-Sat. Closed 2wks Aug. **Average** €. **No credit cards**.
This new-but-old wine and salad bar offers a range of creative salads: radicchio, pine nuts, sultanas and parmesan are all represented. There are also one or two hot pasta or soup dishes, plus crostini with mozzarella and other toppings, and a good selection of crêpes. With its pared-back Roman osteria decor, friendly service and excellently priced wine list, this is a good bet for a cheap, light meal in the heart of the Centro Storico.

Pizzerie

Pizza Ciro
Via della Mercede 43 (06 678 6015). Bus to piazza San Silvestro. **Meals served** 11am-1.30am daily. **Average** €-€€. **Credit** AmEx, DC, MC, V.
From the street this looks like a modest, vaguely touristy pizza parlour, but Ciro is in fact a huge dining factory with 150 seats, many of them in the large back room which also houses the pizza oven. The pizzas – of the high-crust Neapolitan variety – are not at all bad, and the Campanian primi, including tubetti alla Ciro (with rocket and mussels), provide a decent alternative for those who are all doughed out. Sentimental, technicolour Bay of Naples murals set the design tone; the service is brisk but efficient. The best thing about Ciro, though, is the fact that the kitchen keeps going all day, and into the night.

PizzaRé
Via di Ripetta 14 (06 321 1468). Metro Flaminia. **Meals served** 12.45-3.30pm, 7.30pm-12.30am daily. Closed 1wk Aug. **Average** €-€€. **Credit** AmEx, DC, MC, V.
When it opened a few years back, this flagship branch of a chain outlet was one of the leaders of the Neapolitan pizza invasion; sadly, it has not aged well. It offers 40 varieties of high-rise pizzas, various antipasti and a range of salads. But the cheerful Mediterranean decor contrasts with the often surly service, and the rather stodgy pizzas are no good advertisement for the Neapolitan way.

The via Lucullo branch of PizzaRé occupies a Belle Epoque villa with a garden patio for summer dining. (via Lucullo 22; 06 4201 3075).

Opera Unica
Via del Leone 23 (06 6880 9927). Bus to via Tomacelli. **Meals served** 12.30-3pm, 7.30-11pm Mon-Sat; 7.30-11pm Sun. Closed 3wks Aug. **Average** €€. **Credit** AmEx, DC, MC, V.

This place gives itself airs – perhaps because it's just across the square from the Circolo della Caccia (Hunt Club), haunt of the Roman aristocracy. But a fairly ordinary pizzeria lurks behind the façade of linen tablecloths, jazzy menus, stencilled ceiling patterns and dangly lampshades. The decent but overpriced pizzas – more Roman than Neapolitan – range from the standard (margherita) to the more recherché (buffalo mozzarella with courgette flowers). There is also a small range of salads, promising on paper but lame in execution. Orders are taken by bored-looking waiters with electronic pen gadgets. And the beer is warm.

International

Hamasei
Via della Mercede 35/36 (06 679 2134). Bus to piazza San Silvestro. **Meals served** noon-2.30pm, 7-10.30pm Tue-Sun. Closed 1wk Aug. **Average** €€-€€€. **Credit** AmEx, DC, MC, V.
A branch of a famous Tokyo eaterie, this is Rome's most traditional Japanese restaurant, oozing oriental elegance and packed with a reassuringly large slice of Rome's stable or visiting Japanese population. Explore the sushi, sashimi or sukiyaki, served at candlelit tables. Lunch is a good time to try the place out: there are four fixed lunch menus, all priced at €13. In the evening, count on paying at least €30 a head.

Le Pain Quotidien
Via Tomacelli 24/25 (06 6880 7727). Bus to via Tomacelli. **Meals served** 9am-midnight Tue-Sun. **Average** €€. **Credit** AmEx, DC, MC, V.
Rome is nowhere near as susceptible to the multinational dining franchise as some other European capitals. But the first Italian outlet of this Belgian chain – which has also opened in New York – has been a resounding success. The shelves of stone-ground bread and white-capped doughboys are a backdrop to the main act, which is the feeding of hordes around huge, communal wooden tables. Salads, cheese platters and pâtés dominate the menu, which is supplemented on weekends by the latest Roman fighetto (rich kid) craze: the American brunch.

Wine bars & pubs

Antica Enoteca di Via della Croce
Via della Croce 76B (06 679 0896). Metro Spagna/bus to via Tomacelli. **Open** 11.30am-1am daily. **Average** €€. **Credit** AmEx, DC, MC, V.

Achille Enoteca al Parlamento (via dei Prefetti 15) is a high-class bottle shop with a good range of wines by the glass.

Le Pain Quotidien

When this place opened in 1842 it was the favourite haunt
of Scandinavian painters who lived on Via Margutta. A
tasteful revamp has retained most of the original fittings,
including the marble wine vats and a venerable wooden
cash desk. There's a good selection of wines by the glass,
plus a cold buffet at the counter and a restaurant with
tables in the long back room offering a full range of hot
dishes at meal times. It also operates as an off licence.

Buccone

*Via di Ripetta 19 (06 361 2154). Metro Flaminio/bus to
piazza del Popolo.* **Open** *Restaurant* 12.30-3pm Mon-Thur;
12.30-3pm, 7.30-11pm Fri, Sat. *Wine bar/shop* 9am-8.30pm
Mon-Thur; 9am-midnight Fri, Sat. Closed 3wks Aug.
Average €. **Credit** AmEx, DC, MC, V.
This historic osteria at the piazza del Popolo end of via di
Ripetta began life in the 18th century as a carriage garage
for aristocrats. For years it operated as an off licence with
a few wines available by the glass at the marble counter;
but recently tables have been arranged among the high
wooden shelves. There are always three or four pasta
dishes or soups, followed by a range of meaty seconds and
creative salads. The cooking is more than competent, the
prices extremely reasonable and the service friendly.

Il Brillo Parlante

*Via della Fontanella 12 (06 323 5017/www.
ilbrilloparlante.com). Metro Flaminio/bus to piazza del
Popolo.* **Open** *Bar* 11am-2am Tue-Sun. *Restaurant* 12.30-
3.30pm, 7.30pm-1am Tue-Sat; 7.30pm-1am Sun. Closed
3wks Aug. **Average** €€. **Credit** AmEx, DC, MC, V.

In the entrance bar, you can drink wines by the glass; downstairs, this wine bar around the corner from piazza del Popolo opens out into a low, vaulted cellar, with obtrusive ventilation ducts and heraldic frescoes. Unusually for a wine bar, it does pizzas – although not exactly the best in town – as well as some surprisingly creative pasta dishes, such as asparagus-filled ravioli served with castelmagno cheese and toasted almonds. Good for a one-course gourmet meal on the run.

Caffè: a user's guide

In Italy, coffee is a sacred drug. It has little to do with what is passed off as Italian coffee in the chain cafés of London and New York. Variety always proliferates where the anchor of tradition has been lost, and no Italian would be seen dead drinking a mochaccino, let alone a cappuccino flavoured with cinammon or orange. If you want to earn respect from the local coffee posse, here are some guidelines.

Get your receipt first, then slap it down on the counter.

As much as you might want to, don't ask for 'un espresso'; a short, black coffee here is simply 'un caffè'.

Never drink cappuccino, or any milky beverage, after meals. Italians dislike the idea of milk on a full stomach, and ordering a cappuccino after lunch is the cultural equivalent of asking for a cup of tea in a pub.

If you want caffè macchiato, there's no need to specify this at the till as it costs the same.

Don't order a coffee at the bar and then take it to a table, unless you are a regular: you pay extra for the privilege of sitting down.

Coffee comes in a strictly limited series of variations on the basic, black espresso and the basic, frothy cappuccino. The main versions are: caffè ristretto – with hardly any water; caffè lungo – with a little more water than the basic caffè; caffè Americano – extremely diluted; caffè macchiato – with a dash of milk (either freddo – cold – or caldo – hot and frothy, cappuccino-style); caffè doppio – double-strength coffee (more of a tourist thing; Italians tend to pace their caffeine intake), caffè corretto – with a dash of rum, cognac or whisky; caffe latte – half milk/half coffee; and latte macchiato – hot milk with a dash of coffee.

If you don't want the caffeine, ask for a decaf (caffè hag) or caffè d'orzo (barley coffee). In summer, caffè freddo and cappuccino freddo are popular iced coffee variants. These generally come pre-sugared: if you want yours without, ask for it amaro (literally, 'bitter').

There are also a few permutations on the way coffee is served, in particular, ordering your coffee 'al vetro' (in a glass) is a very Roman thing to do.

Shaki

Via Mario de Fiori 29A (06 679 1694). Metro Spagna.
Open *Mar-Sept* 9.30am-midnight daily. *Oct-Feb* 10.30am-
10.30pm daily. **Average** €€. **Credit** AmEx, DC, MC, V.
In the middle of the fashion triangle, this ultra-stylish
wine bar, which opened in March 2001, looks like it has
landed from some distant planet (that is, Milan). Design
is cool, modern and faintly Japanese; but the food is
unrepentantly Mediterranean. There are no hot dishes,
only a selection of panini and salads made with fresh
ingredients. Prices are on the high side for what's on offer:
a filled roll (such as the Portofino, with salmon, rocket
and pesto) and a glass of white Tocai will set you back
€13: look at it as a subsidy for the waiters' haircuts.

Bars & Cafés

Antico Caffè Greco

Via Condotti 86 (06 679 1700). Metro Spagna. **Open** 8am-
8.30pm daily. Closed 1wk Aug. **Credit** AmEx, DC, MC, V.
Founded in 1760, this venerable café was the one-time
hangout of Casanova, Goethe, Wagner, Stendhal,
Baudelaire, Shelley and Byron, and became a centre of
underground nationalist resistance during the French
occupation of Rome in 1849-70. These days it has a split
personality – the sofas out the back are packed with
tourists, while local office and fashion staff cram the bar,
where an excellent espresso is served. Literary and
musical evenings hark back to its artistic past.

Babington's

Piazza di Spagna 23 (06 678 6027). Metro Spagna. **Open**
9am-8.15pm Mon, Wed-Sun. **Credit** AmEx, DC, MC, V.
Britons may not consider visiting tea rooms abroad a
priority, but will often be directed here by well-meaning
Romans, convinced that they cannot survive without an
overpriced pot of tea and plate of cakes. Founded by two
British spinsters, Babington's has been around since the
late 19th century, and it shows. Considering its exorbitant
prices, the surroundings are down-at-heel. The menu
offers a wide selection of teas from around the world,
ranging from €7 for a small pot to an absurd €30 for more
exotic selections. Since the most reasonably priced items
on the menu are the long drinks at €10, we recommend
you overlook the teas and treat yourself to a stiff one.

Café Notegen

*Via del Babuino 159 (06 320 0855). Metro Spagna/bus to
via del Babuino.* **Open** 7.30am-1am daily. **Credit** AmEx,
DC, MC, V.

Babington's
See p45.

A historic gathering spot for theatre people, artists and intellectuals, this 19th-century café prides itself on being a 'café in the French sense', serving hot and cold Roman and international dishes and great cakes at any hour to a wide range of homely locals and literary flâneurs. Downstairs, cabaret, music (with dancing) and the odd play are offered on a rather irregular basis.

Caffetteria La Barcaccia

Piazza di Spagna 71 (06 679 7497). Metro Spagna. **Open** *Oct-Mar* 7am-9pm daily. *Apr-Sept* 8am-midnight daily. **Credit** AmEx, DC, MC, V.
Right up the street from Prada, Bulgari and Gucci, this is a good place to recuperate and regroup after an exhausting day's shopping. Upstairs, there's a pleasant, airy tea room for relaxing over a sandwich or slice of cake.

Canova

Piazza del Popolo 16 (06 361 2231). Metro Flaminio/bus to piazza del Popolo. **Open** 8am-midnight daily. **Credit** AmEx, DC, MC, V.
Traditionally, Canova's clientele has always dressed (and voted) to the right, shunning the leftie intellectuals that hang out at **Rosati** (*see p48*) across the square. But the days of those heady cultural stand-offs are long past, and today the main reason for patronising this increasingly tatty, characterless bar is that it catches the late afternoon sun. And maybe because on summer evenings it stays open into the small hours.

The wine bar Shaki (*see p45*) has a designer food and lifestyle shop at piazza di Spagna 65 (06 678 6605).

Ciampini al Café du Jardin

Viale Trinità dei Monti (06 678 5678). Metro Spagna.
Open *Mar-May, Oct, Nov* 8am-8pm daily. *June-Sept* 8am-
1am Mon, Tue, Thur-Sun. Closed mid Nov-mid Mar.
Credit AmEx, DC, MC, V.

This open-air café is surrounded by creeper-curtained
trellises, with a pretty pond in the centre. It serves a
selection of tasty sandwiches, pastas, cocktails, ices,
snack lunches and filling breakfasts; the evening menu
(June-Sept) is more substantial. The view over the
rooftops of Rome is stunning, especially at sunset.

Dolci e Doni

*Via delle Carrozze 85B (06 6992 5001). Metro
Spagna/bus to via del Corso.* **Open** 9am-midnight daily.
Closed 2wks Aug. **Credit** AmEx, DC, MC, V.

A tiny, bijou tea room, renowned for its cakes and
chocolates, Dolci e Doni has recently expanded its menu
to include not only breakfasts, and quiche and salad
lunches, but also upmarket hot dishes such as goose
breast and quails' eggs. Cakes can be taken away, and
staff will also arrange catering for parties.

Elen Bar

*Via Capo le Case 27 (06 679 3987). Metro Spagna/bus to
piazza San Silvestro.* **Open** 6am-7.30pm Mon-Sat. **Credit**
MC, V.

This tiny daytime bar makes a great breakfast or lunch
stop. The rolls and salads are fresh and tasty, as are the
centrifughe – juiced shakes of carrot, apple, pineapple,
etc. Desserts consist of own-made crostate and fruit
salads. The family that runs the place extends a welcome
that is rare in offhand Rome, and there's no extra charge
for table service – not even for the single outside table,
which is keenly contested by local office workers.

Gran Caffè La Caffetteria

Via Margutta 61A (06 321 3344). Metro Spagna. **Open**
10am-9pm Tue-Sun. Closed 3wks Aug. **Credit** AmEx,
MC, V.

This huge café occupies a 17th-century theatre on artsy
via Margutta. Inside is a warren of rooms, with decor
ranging from 18th century (including original frescoes on
the cross-beamed ceilings) to art nouveau. There's no
crush at the counter: just understated (and a trifle
overpriced) waiter service.

La Buvette

Via Vittoria 44 (06 679 0383). Metro Spagna/bus to via del Babuino. **Open** 7.30am-2am Mon-Sat. Closed 2wks Aug. **Credit** AmEx, DC, MC, V.

All polished wood and mirrors, the Buvette serves some decent coffee and cakes in plush, cosy surroundings. A couple of pasta dishes and a wide range of salads are also served (lunch only between June and September, lunch and dinner for the rest of the year). The lower level features a rather stuffy restaurant; the upstairs bar is much more rewarding.

Mercedes Café

Via delle Convertite 19 (06 6929 2915). Bus to piazza San Silvestro. **Open** 7am-9pm Mon-Sat. Closed 2 wks Aug. **Credit** AmEx, DC, MC, V.

On the corner of the busy bus and shopping hub of piazza San Silvestro, this recently opened café offers a slick, stainless steel and bleached wood take on the traditional Roman bar. Apart from breakfast cappuccino, the smartly aproned young staff serve snacks at lunchtime (there's a small restaurant upstairs) and a whole range of complimentary nibbles from 7pm to 9pm for the aperitivo set. As the name suggests, the adjoining Mercedes outlet promotes all the necessary in-house merchandise, from key rings to T-shirts.

Rosati ★

Piazza del Popolo 5 (06 322 5859). Metro Flaminio/bus to piazza del Popolo. **Open** 7.45am-11.30pm daily. **Credit** AmEx, DC, MC, V.

Rosati is the traditional haunt of Rome's intellectual left: Calvino, Moravia and Pasolini were regulars. Rosati's barmen are among the city's best mixers and shakers; try their Sogni Romani cocktail: an orange juice and liqueur symphony in red and yellow – the colours of the city. The cakes and cornetti are baked on the premises, and the sandwiches are a cut above the Roman standard. American-style brunch is served on Sundays (1-4pm) between October and mid-March.

Vitti

Piazza di San Lorenzo in Lucina 33 (06 687 6304). Bus to via del Corso. **Open** 7am-10pm daily. **Credit** AmEx, DC, MC, V.

Of the three bars with tables outside on this pleasant, wedge-shaped piazza just off via del Corso, Vitti has the surest sense of style, and the best view of the church of San Lorenzo in Lucina. It also does great coffee and knockout southern Italian cakes – including babà (a mini-sponge cake soaked in rum) and the dazzling cassatina (a smaller version of the Sicilian cassata, with marzipan, ricotta and chocolate chips).

Navona

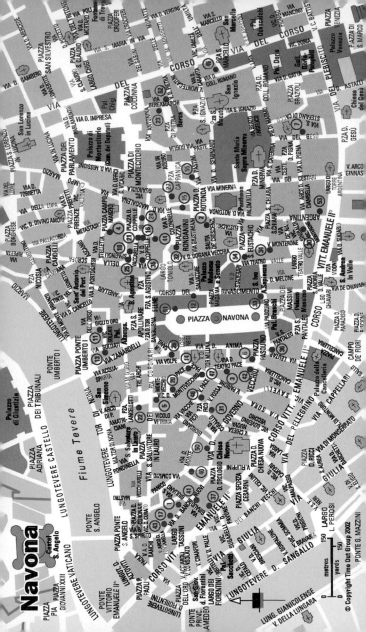

Officially, the Centro Storico is the whole area inside the Aurelian walls. But in common parlance, the term is often used to refer to the area defined and enclosed by the central Tiber bend. Sparsely populated in classical times, what is today a high-density tourist destination was built up in the Middle Ages and the Renaissance to process pilgrims and coddle cardinals. Artisans and courtesans lived side by side with Rome's wealthy families. Today, it seems little has changed. Wandering the streets here you are as likely to see a gattara (cat lady) as a penthouse-dwelling politician or film director.

Navona

Restaurants

Alfredo e Ada ★

Via dei Banchi Nuovi 14 (06 687 8842). Bus to corso Vittorio Emanuele (Chiesa Nuova). **Meals served** 1-3.30pm, 8-10.30pm Mon-Fri. Closed Aug, 1wk Dec-Jan. **Average** €. **No credit cards**.
After a morning's sightseeing in the Vatican, cross over Ponte Sant'Angelo for a nostalgia trip back into the popular Rome of black and white films courtesy of Zia (Aunt) Ada, who has been bustling among this restaurant's eight tables since the 1940s. The day's set-price menu is chalked on a board; it generally includes simple dishes such as spaghetti aglio e olio (in garlic and olive oil) and spezzatino di vitello con piselli (veal stew with peas) or salsiccia con fagioli (sausage with beans). Dessert consists of a plateful of home-made biscuits that Zia Ada fishes out of a battered tin box. She does not serve coffee: in any case, there is no time for it, as the waiting hordes are hungrily eyeing your table. Expect to pay around €17 a head.

Armando al Pantheon

Salita de' Crescenzi 31 (06 6880 3034). Bus or tram to largo Argentina/bus to corso Rinascimento. **Meals served** 12.30-3pm, 7.30-11pm Mon-Fri; 12.30-3pm Sat. Closed Aug. **Average** €€. **Credit** AmEx, DC, MC, V.
It's been here for years, and may it be with us for many more. Armando is a simple, no-frills trattoria a few yards from the Pantheon that has all the marks of authenticity: cork walls, indifferent artworks going back to the 1950s

Bloom

and beyond, a pretty stained-glass entrance. The menu is almost unchanging (we can vouch personally for the past 18 years), with classics like fettuccine all'Armando (with mushrooms, peas and tomatoes) or ossobuco (veal shin stewed in wine and tomatoes) done reliably but with little pretension to the major league. The only concessions to changing times are a few (not always successful) vegetarian dishes added from time to time. Service is friendly, the wine list small but navigable.

Bloom

Via del Teatro Pace 29 (06 6880 2029). Bus to corso Vittorio Emanuele (piazza Navona). **Meals served** 8pm-midnight Mon-Sat. Closed 3wks Aug. **Average** €€€. **Credit** AmEx, DC, MC, V.

Bloom, one of Rome's new wave of fusion eateries, is so stylish it hurts. Its location – in a quiet medieval lane – and its design-heavy entrance bar set the place apart from the snackbar and pizzeria plebs that cluster around piazza Navona. Downstairs is the main restaurant, upstairs the sushi bar; in between, on the staircase, a DJ mixes ambient sounds. As a restaurant, rather than a place to be seen in, Bloom fails on a number of counts. There is no wine list; the waiter we talked to confused Sauvignon with Traminer and seemed to have no clear idea of what was in the cellar. The menu follows the fusion creed, but with no great sense of assurance: a 'soft taco' starter turned out to be a perfectly ordinary crêpe,

Pralineria

Enoteca

'Gusto

Libreria
enoculinaria

Live Music

Ristorante

Pizzeria

Wine Bar

Ristorante *'Gusto* Roma
Piazza Augusto Imperatore, 9
Via della Frezza, 23
Telefono 063226273
www.gusto.it

while the trofiette al pesto di noci pecan, basilico e menta (pasta with pecan, basil and mint pesto) was, beneath the bird's-nest swirl of its presentation, a rustic dish with slightly overcooked pasta. Things looked up with the dessert of bavarese al te verde con crema alla cannella (green tea bavarois with cinammon sauce) – but at €12 a throw, so they should. If the prices were cheaper, the hit and miss approach (which, on our last visit, extended to the billing) wouldn't really matter. But there are far better meals to be had in the city for this price.

Boccondivino ★

Piazza Campo Marzio 6 (06 6830 8626). Bus to piazza San Silvestro. **Meals served** 12.30-3pm, 7.30-11.30pm Mon-Sat. **Average** €€€. **Credit** AmEx, DC, MC, V.
This place is a convincing attempt to combine design flair with culinary excellence. The entrance, flanked by two columns from an ancient Roman temple to Mars, gives on to a jazzy space with faux marble walls, a creeper-forest of high tech lights and zebra-striped wire bucket chairs. The food's stylish too: Boccondivino's mod-Med fusion approach comes through in a cilindro di calamari su purea di patate all'olio e bottarga di muggine (squid on a bed of potatoes mashed in oil with mullet bottarga), or in the petto di anatra con verdure caramellate e salsa al miele (duck breast with caramelised vegetables and honey sauce). Dinner is à la carte, but at lunch there's a good-value two-course business menu – more traditional Italian than fusion – which is offered with mineral water and wine at €18. On our last visit, the bumbling waiters looked as if they had been hired for the evening – but as it was a public holiday, they probably had.

Cantina del Vecchio

Via dei Coronari 30 (06 686 7427). Bus to via Zanardelli. **Meals served** 7.30-11.30pm Mon; 12.30-2.30pm, 7.30-11.30pm Tue-Sat. Closed 2wks Jan, 2wks Aug. **Average** €€€. **Credit** AmEx, DC, MC, V.
Via dei Coronari is lined with antique shops, and this warm, romantic restaurant, housed on the ground floor of a 16th-century palazzo, enters fully into the spirit of the neighbourhood. With its wood panelling, antique grandfather clock and ornate chandelier, it exudes elegance, and the only sound that disturbs an evening meal is cocktails being shaken at the bar. The food, however, divided equally between classic Italian dishes and Roman staples revisited, is less exalted. A saltimbocca d'orata con insalata di carciofi e finocchio (sea bream 'saltimbocca' with artichoke and fennel) was bone-dry, sauceless and served without the promised fennel, and the restaurant's nouveau version of rigatoni all'amatriciana doesn't meet the standards of even the

grittiest Roman osteria. The beef fillet on a bed of red-wine-braised radicchio and pancetta-wrapped prunes made for a nice marriage of flavours, but the fois gras with which it claimed to be stuffed was nowhere to be found. There's no faulting the desserts, though – especially the outstanding strudel of apples, raisins and pine nuts with cinnamon ice-cream.

Ciccia Bomba

Via del Governo Vecchio 76 (06 6880 2108). Bus to corso Vittorio Emanuele (piazza Navona). **Meals served** 12.30-3pm, 7.30-11.30pm Mon, Tue, Thur-Sun. Closed 2wks Aug. **Average** €€. **Credit** AmEx, DC, MC, V.

A leisurely meander from piazza Navona brings you to this traditional Roman trattoria. Service is quick and no nonsense, and the food is reliable (and, given the location, decently priced). The menu follows ancient Roman culinary patterns, offering, for instance, trippa all Romana (stewed tripe) on Saturdays and gnocchi on Thursdays. More adventurous dishes include radicchio trevigiano e formaggio alla griglia (grilled red chicory with melted cheese). Pizzas are available in the evenings. Lunchtimes are not a problem, but book ahead for dinner.

Enoteca Corsi ★

Via del Gesu 87-8 (06 679 0821). Bus to piazza Venezia/bus or tram to largo Argentina. **Meals served** noon-3pm Mon-Sat. Closed Aug. **Average** €. **Credit** AmEx, DC, MC, V.

This old 1940s wine shop has expanded to take in a noisy lunch crowd, who come for home cooking at very reasonable prices. The daily menu is written up on the board at the entrance. If you need a translation, ask for Ilaria – though getting anyone's attention can be quite a task. Do as the locals do: shout above the din and get in your order before the most popular dishes run out. The kitchen follows the traditional Roman weekly calendar – so it's gnocchi on Thursdays, and on Fridays baccalà (salt cod) in various ways – try it alla livornese, with onion and tomato sauce. If you are still hungry, a slice of ricotta tart followed by an espresso, or tozzetti (Tuscan almond biscuits) with vin santo, make a fitting end to a hearty meal. For a more relaxing lunch, the furthest room at the back is the quieter, original and still-operating wine shop.

Il Bacaro

Via degli Spagnoli 27 (06 686 4110). Bus to corso Rinascimento. **Meals served** 12.30-2.30pm, 8-11.30pm Mon-Fri; 8-11.30pm Sat. Closed 3wks Jan-Feb. **Average** €€€. **Credit** DC, MC, V.

Although there's no space to swing the proverbial spaghetto, this tiny eaterie, located in a maze of alleys behind the Pantheon, manages to serve up an interesting

One of the best places for a snack lunch in the Centro Storico, **Fratelli Paladini** (via del Governo Vecchio 29) does delicious, oven-hot pizza bianca, filled with various goodies. Be prepared to queue.

Boccondivino. *See p55.*

selection of dishes. For first courses, thumbs up to the risotto con Castelmagno e vino rosso (risotto with Castelmagno cheese and red wine) and gnocchi con Roquefort e noci (walnuts), while the filetto di manzo al Merlot (fillet steak in a red wine sauce) and stracetti di filetto all'aceto balsamico con rughetta e grana (thin strips of beef cooked in balsamic vinegar and served with rocket and cheese) are less exciting follow-ups. The wine list has nice surprises and the double-chocolate mousse di cioccolato con cioccolato caldo is stellar.

Il Convivio ★

Vicolo dei Soldati 31 (06 686 9432/www.ilconvivio troiani.com). Bus to corso Rinascimento. **Meals served** 8-10.30pm Mon; 1-2.30pm, 8-10.30pm Tue-Sat. Closed 1wk Aug. **Average** €€€€€. **Credit** AmEx, DC, MC, V.
The three Troiani brothers run a high-class act in this temple of foodie excellence just north of piazza Navona.

The first of the three elegant, vaulted rooms is for those who enjoy watching waiter traffic; the other two, with chiaroscuro murals and dark oil paintings, are more intimate. The menu changes with the season and the latest experiments of chef Angelo. His creative approach is rooted in the tradition of his native Marches, where fresh vegetables, meat, game and seafood all take equal billing. An antipasto of polpettine di seppia con carciofo alla romana (cuttlefish rissoles with Roman-style artichoke) is a good example of his approach: a dish from the popular tradition brought into sharp relief by the addition of something a little nouvelle. Among the primi, a dish of vermicelli bucati di Gragnano all'amatriciana sfumati al balsamico (long pasta tubes with tomato, cured pork jowl, pecorino and a touch of balsamic vinegar) is a revelation, while the main course piccione arrostito alla salvia e pepe rosa, tortino di radicchio, salsa di vino rosso (pigeon roasted in sage and pink peppercorns, with

Enoteca Corsi. *See p56.*

braised radicchio in red wine sauce) offers a nice balance between sweet, rich and piquant flavours. Desserts are up to the same standard: the classic semifreddo di zabaione con mandorle pralinate e aceto balsamico (zabaione ice-cream with praline almonds and balsamic vinegar) will put you off Haagen-Dazs for life. The cellar is extensive, with a wide range of non-Italian labels. Mark-ups are steep on cheaper bottles, less severe on more classy ones, so you might as well push the boat out and finish up with a fine selection of rums and distillati.

Il Cantuccio

Corso Rinascimento 71 (06 6880 2982). Bus to corso Rinascimento. **Meals served** 12.30-3.30pm, 7.30pm-2am Mon-Sat. Closed Aug, 1wk Jan. **Average** €€€. **Credit** AmEx, DC, MC, V.
If your idea of fun is dining out with Italian politicians and their bodyguards, or watching TV starlets greet each other in a flurry of air-kissing, then Il Cantuccio is a must.

The low lighting, candles, mirrors and pink tablecloths give it a sort of claustrophobic, retro-nightclub feel, enhanced by the framed photos of film stars hung on the walls. But the service has verve, and you can get a table well after midnight. Familiar Italian dishes are given original twists: pasta e patate (pasta and potato soup) comes with a flavouring of pecorino e bottarga (pecorino cheese and fish roe), while spaghetti al pecorino is served in a focaccia case. There are also more traditional dishes such as the rombo in crosta di patate, olive e pomodorini (turbot in potato crust, with olives and cherry tomatoes). The grilled vegetable platter drizzled with olive oil makes a perfect second course for vegetarians or light diners. If you can't face the profiteroles or crêpes with chocolate sauce, there are after-dinner biscuits and sweet wine.

Il Primoli

Via dei Soldati 22-3 (06 6813 5277). Bus to corso Rinascimento. **Meals served** 12.30-3pm, 8.30pm-midnight Mon-Fri; 8.30pm-midnight Sat. Closed Aug. **Average** €€€. **Credit** AmEx, DC, MC, V.

Housed in the centuries-old palazzo of the same name, this restaurant has a spare, clean look with all the modern elements you'd expect to find in an upscale London restaurant – hardwood floors, grey-on-white tables, brushed chrome ceiling fixtures. All the elements combine to give a modern appeal to a space that is larger than it seems from the street. The creative Italian menu with international leanings reads well, although the food doesn't always live up to the promise. The misto di marinati in salsa di aceto balsamico e frutta (mixed marinated fish in balsamic dressing with fruit) is enlivened by fresh fruit confetti, and the plate is pretty enough. But a primo of mezzelune alle castagne e fois gras de canard (half-moon ravioli stuffed with chestnuts in a foie gras sauce) was dry, and the pasta itself much too thick. A secondo of wild boar goulash was tasty and nicely spiced, but the rice it came with clearly needed another ten minutes' boiling time. Desserts are slightly more impressive, but the wine list is rather limited.

La Focaccia

Via della Pace 11 (06 6880 3312). Bus to corso Vittorio Emanuele. **Meals served** *Oct-Apr* noon-4pm, 7pm-12.30am daily. *May-Sept* noon-12.30am daily. **Average** €€. **Credit** MC, V.

This funky trattoria on a fashionable but still charming lane west of piazza Navona has a downstairs dining room and bar awash in greens and blues, plus, in the warmer months, tables out front. The bustling environment is the backdrop for some very worthwhile simple Italian cooking. Among the starters, zeppole (fried dough fritters) offer an alternative to the traditional baked

Though service is snooty and prices steep, the calorie-bomb tartufi (chocolate ice-cream balls larded with lumps of dark chocolate) purveyed by **I Tre Scalini** (piazza Navona 28-32) are well worth a try.

bruschette, while the fusilli gragnano al curry e broccoli con pinoli (corkscrew pasta with curry, broccoli and pine nuts) is one of the more creative pasta options on offer here. A melt-in-the-mouth veal stew with roasted potatoes hits the spot on cold nights, and takes you away from pasta for a little while. The staff are young, friendly and English-speaking, and the long opening hours are a helpful and unexpected bonus.

La Rosetta

Via della Rosetta 8-9 (06 686 1002/www.larosetta.com). *Bus to via del Corso.* **Meals served** 12.45-2.45pm, 7.45-11.30pm Mon-Fri; 7.45-11.30pm Sat. Closed 2wks Aug. **Average** €€€€€. **Credit** AmEx, DC, MC, V.

It has to be admitted that La Rosetta is one of the best seafood restaurants in town, but be warned – the prices are punishing. The Gran Misto di antipasti (€32) – a huge selection of starters like carpaccio of tuna marinated in thyme – gives you a chance to sample what the restaurant does best: squeaky-fresh, top-quality fish, prepared in a way that makes a virtue of simplicity. It is standard practice to follow this up with a primo like spaghetti with scampi and courgette flowers – a house speciality, cooked with a good deal of chili – or rigatoni con cernia, pomodoro fresco e menta (pasta with sea bass, fresh tomato and mint), and then skip the main course altogether. In summer, opt for the elegant, vaguely nautical, air-conditioned interior rather than one of the cramped pavement tables. The only drawback is the uncomfortable seats and vaguely smarmy service, which is hardly what one expects for this kind of money.

The best cheap lunch

Margutta Vegetariano Ristorante
See p38.

Vic's
See p41.

Caffetteria Borromini
See p118.

Enoteca Corsi
See p56.

Le Pain Quotidien
See p42.

BAR & GRILL
open every day
on Saturday and on Sunday
SPECIAL BRUNCH

Via del Collegio Romano, 6 - 06. 6786472

 GUINNESS

La Veranda

La Veranda Hotel Columbus - *Borgo Santo Spirito 73*
Roma - Tel: 06-6872973 laveranda@caugest.it

Within the 15th Century building Palazzo della Rovere, in the halls of its ancient refectory and the splendid garden, La Veranda's most creative and professional chefs and sommeliers have reached a high quality standard in catering. The Italian gastronomy in all its different expressions from the most traditional to the most creative one, conveys all the characteristics of a high quality restaurant to the organisation of different kinds of events, through an attentive selection of Mediterranean products.

Rex

Rex Hotel Rex - *Via Torino 149 Roma - Tel: 06-4815702/06-4824828*
info.fh@caugest.it

Expertise in the wine, cooking and food industry make the Rex the right place for a quick but very high quality catering service, the result of a search for Italian products proposed during gastronomic and didactic meetings aimed at testing different typical products. This is how some events like GIOREX, SAYCHEESE and the CIGARBAR have come about. They all have the particularity of being "amusing experiments" linked to food and wine.

Maccheroni

Piazza delle Coppelle 44 (06 6830 7895). Bus to corso Rinascimento. **Meals served** 1-3pm, 8pm-midnight Mon-Sat. **Average** €€. **Credit** AmEx, MC, V.

This young, funky eaterie, which opened in 1998, is already an established favourite with trendy locals, visiting celebrities and actresses who are just about to make it big. In summer, tables spill out on to the pretty square. Inside, boathouse-style panelled walls and long marble counters separate the eating area from the open-to-view kitchens. The food is basic trattoria fare, served distractedly by young waiters. The antipasto selection of cold meats and cheeses is tasty enough, but if you are persuaded to order it 'for the whole table,' you *will* be charged for the whole table. As its name suggests, pasta is Maccheroni's's forte: the trofie al tartufo nero (short pasta twists in truffle cream sauce) are heavenly, as are the gnocchi with pear and gorgonzola. The basic secondi can be disappointing; the only one that stands out is the mouth-watering grilled steak, either served whole or sliced on a bed of rocket.

Miró

Via dei Banchi Nuovi 8 (06 6880 8527). Bus to corso Vittorio Emanuele (Chiesa Nuova). **Meals served** 7.30-11.30pm Mon, Wed-Sun. Closed 3wks Aug. **Average** €€. **Credit** AmEx, DC, MC, V.

This warm and welcoming Calabrian restaurant is surprisingly spacious. A long, narrow corridor leads into a series of rooms with the rose-coloured vaulted ceilings of a Renaissance palazzo. When you reserve, be sure to ask for the bucatini fatto a mano (handmade thick, hollow spaghetti), which the kitchen prepares by request only. Fish is always fresh, and the involtini al vino bianco (rolled veal with cheese sautéd in white wine) is superb. The kitchen stays open reasonably late, so it can be a good bet for an after-movie meal.

Montevecchio

Piazza Montevecchio 22A (06 686 1319). Bus to via Zanardelli. **Meals served** 7.30-11.30pm Tue-Sun. Closed 3wks Jan, 1wk Aug. **Average** €€€. **Credit** DC, MC, V.

Little piazza Montevecchio is bathed in sunny charm or austere gloom, depending on the time of day. The area has become a bit of a culinary magnet recently, but this small corner restaurant predates the gold rush. With its white walls, red velvet chairs, Arcadian artworks and dungeon grates, Montevecchio has something of the cardinal's residence about it. The food also seems designed to appeal to international clerical palates; though undoubtedly competent, it has a little too much of the hotel restaurant about it. An antipasto of terrina di

ceci con capesante, olive, pinoli ed olio al rosmarino
(terrine of chickpeas with scallops, olives, pine nuts, and
rosemary-flavoured oil) was a little tired, as was a Gallic-
style primo of gnocchi soufflé ai carciofi (a 'soufflé' of
gnocchi with artichokes, that had precious little of the
soufflé about it). Secondi range from fish – including a
decent rombo in crosta di mandorle (turbot in an almond
jacket) – to meat and game. Desserts include a succulent,
comforting terrina calda di frutti di bosco (warm wild
fruit terrine), served in a zabaione sauce, based on vino
passito (dessert wine) from the island of Pantelleria.
Service is attentive, but there's little atmosphere, despite
the baroque classical soundtrack, and prices are
decidedly high for what's on offer.

Myosotis

Vicolo della Vaccarella 3-5 (06 686 5554). Bus to
corso Rinascimento. **Meals served** 12.30-3pm,
7.30-11pm Mon-Sat. Closed 2-3wks Aug. **Average** €€€.
Credit AmEx, DC, MC, V.
Myosotis was one of the first of a 1990s generation of
Centro Storico trattorie offering updated versions of
Italian classics using home-grown or handmade
ingredients. True to its origins, it continues to deliver the
goods, from the house antipasto of mozzarella, ricotta,
focaccia and stuffed pimento to the vellutata di ceci e
porcini (chickpea and porcini soup). Carnivores will
appreciate the gnocchetti al castrato (small gnocchi with
a mutton ragu), although fish is also a good bet,
particularly the frittura di paranza (small, deep-fried fish
and seafood). Top marks go to the honest mark-ups on
wines and the friendly and efficient service, though, on
the other hand, it's fair to say that the pink-on-pink decor
isn't the best aid to digestion.

Osteria dell'Antiquario

Piazzetta di San Simeone 26-7 (06 687 9694). Bus to
via Zanardelli. **Meals served** 12.30-2.30pm, 8-11pm
Mon-Sat. Closed 2wks Jan, 1wk Aug. **Average** €€€.
Credit AmEx, DC, MC, V.
This is the best of the restaurants on antique-ridden via
dei Coronari. The menu balances the chef's experimental
forays with dishes from the Roman tradition. Fish is a
strong point; an antipasto of salmone marinato al
coriandolo con funghi, rughetta e caviale (salmon
marinated in coriander, mushroom, rocket and caviar) is
a delight. Unusually for Rome, there is also a wide
selection of cheeses, including roquefort con miele di
castagna (roquefort with chestnut honey). The desserts,
such as mousse alle pere e noci con salsa all'arancia
(mousse with pears and walnuts in an orange sauce) are
spectacular. The food more than makes up for the

Sangallo

*Vicolo della Vaccarella 11A (06 686 5549). Bus to corso
Rinascimento.* **Meals served** 7.30-10.30pm Mon-Sat.
Closed Aug. **Average** €€€€. **Credit** AmEx, DC, MC, V.
Roman seafood maven Gianfranco Panattoni comes from
the nearby port of Anzio. He is a fast-talking gourmet
with an extensive wine list and a talent for melding the
day's catch with locally sourced fruit and vegetables.
Antipasti such as a carpaccio of red bream, king prawns,
shrimp, orange and olives, or artichokes stuffed with
calamari segue into primi like cannolicchi (shell-shaped
pasta) with clams, peppers, cherry tomatoes and spicy
salame, which might be followed by a delicate fillet of sea
bass with porcini mushrooms. Unfortunately, while the
kitchen mostly gets it right, the same cannot be said for
the service. It is not unusual to wait up to an hour before
giving your order and taking your first bite. Complaints
about wine orders being mishandled are fairly common
here. Still, on its good nights, Sangallo can be very good
indeed: just make sure you're not in a hurry.

Santa Lucia

*Largo Febo 12 (06 6880 2427). Bus to corso
Rinascimento.* **Meals served** 12.30-3pm, 8pm-midnight
daily. **Average** €€€. **Credit** MC, V.
The latest venture of Bar della Pace (*see p76*) founder
Bartolo Cuomo is this late-opening bar/restaurant in largo
Febo, a sweet, shady square next to piazza Navona. The
look here is a stylish collision between a Roman antique
shop and a Moroccan hotel. When weather permits, tables
are arranged out in the raised piazza. The food has a
Neapolitan slant – antipasti like pizzelle (puffy mini-
pizzas) and gattò di patate (potato flan) are followed by
decent seafood and vegetable pasta dishes; most clients
then skip straight to the excellent desserts. Service here
can be uncertain, and prices have crept up recently. Still,
it's frequented by film stars as well as tourists.

Settimio al Pantheon

*Via delle Colonnelle 14 (06 678 9651). Bus to via del
Corso (piazza Colonna).* **Meals served** 12.30-2.30pm,
8-10.30pm Tue-Sat. Closed 3wks Aug. **Average** €€.
Credit AmEx, MC, V.
A classic Roman trattoria near the Pantheon, Settimio is
the pride of its owner (of the same name) who, together
with his wife in the kitchen, has presided over the place
since 1957. A clientele of old habitués includes politicians
from the nearby parliament buildings; over the years,
they have left signatures and comments on the
restaurant's terracotta tiles. It's one of the few places in
Rome to serve a wide range of game – including faraone
(guinea fowl), quaglia (quail), pernice (partridge),

Santa Lucia. *See p67.*

cinghiale (wild boar) and beccaccia (woodcock) – often
accompanied by polenta. Roman dishes are also on hand,
including pappardelle al sugo di caccia (thick, broad
noodles with a gamey meat sauce) and pasta
all'amatriciana. Freshly made desserts include great
semifreddi (ice-cream cakes) alla nocciola (with hazelnut)
and alle castagne (with chestnuts).

Vecchia Locanda
*Vicolo Sinibaldi 2 (06 6880 2831). Bus/tram to largo
Argentina.* **Meals served** 12.30-3pm, 6.30-10.30pm Mon-
Sat. Closed 1wk Dec-Jan. **Average** €€. **Credit** AmEx,
DC, MC, V.
This cute trattoria steps from piazza Argentina has a
dimly lit upstairs dining room and a more lively cantina
downstairs, decorated in blue and marigold with lots of
wine bottles. On offer are basic land and sea staples, each
in a number of variations. An antipasto of San Daniele

prosciutto with buffalo mozzarella makes for a simple but appetising start; but when the kitchen starts getting slightly more creative, the food gets muddled and less convincing. The trofie con mazzancolle, rughetta e pomodorini (pasta twists with prawns, arugula and cherry tomatoes) are well presented and decently cooked – but only the heads of the prawns seemed to make it to the plate. Desserts are competent but unexciting.

Pizzerie

Da Francesco

Piazza del Fico 29 (06 686 4009). Bus to corso Vittorio Emanuele (Chiesa Nuova). **Meals served** noon-3pm, 7pm-1am Mon, Wed-Sun; 7pm-1am Tue. **Average** €. **No credit cards**.
Accept no imitations: Da Francesco is the original Centro Storico pizzeria. No bookings are taken: if you get there

before 8pm, you generally walk right on in; if you get there much after, you join the milling throng. The reasons for its popularity are simple: tasty pizzas, a warm, traditional ambience, friendly service and a range of competent, classic primi and secondi for those who can't face a doughy disc. You often get the distinct feeling that you're being rushed in order to free up the table – and you are – but that's the price you pay for a good bargain dinner in the heart of the city.

Le Cornacchie

Piazza Rondanini 53 (06 6813 4544). Bus to corso Rinascimento. **Meals served** 12.30-3.30pm, 7.30-11.30pm daily. **Average** €€. **Credit** DC, MC, V.

Around the corner from the Pantheon, this vegetarian pizzeria-restaurant serves simple, fresh food in a pleasant, light-filled atmosphere. The walls are covered with watercolour paintings of Roman monuments, and curved leather couches draw you to lean back and take in the scene. Between Monday and Saturday, a €10 lunch buffet takes in a main vegetable or pasta dish (both the asparagus with gorgonzola, and the ratatouille are both tasty), dessert, water and coffee; on Sunday, this becomes a €20 all-you-can-eat brunch. At night, the wood stove is lit and you can select from a range of veggie pizzas.

International

Baires

Corso Rinascimento 1 (06 686 1293). Bus to corso Rinascimento/tram to largo Argentina. **Meals served** noon-3.30pm, 7pm-1am daily. **Average** €€. **Credit** AmEx, DC, MC, V.

This casual carnivorous eaterie offers a decent alternative to yet another plate of pasta. The Argentinian theme is carried through from the decor (dark wooden tables against stucco walls lined with sunny painted ceramic tiles) to the menu, in Italian and Spanish. Most of the food is so-so – among the starters, the classic empanadas (turnovers, filled with meat or corn) are a safe bet. For the main course, stick to the Argentinian beef, served grilled with fried potatoes and a fried egg on top, and a variety of sauces on the side. A small salad and a South American beer will round out what is, on balance, a fairly priced, reasonably appetising trip to the pampas.

L'Eau Vive

Via Monterone 85 (06 6880 1095). Bus or tram to largo Argentina. **Open** 12.30-2.30pm, 7.30-10.30pm Mon-Sat. Closed Aug. **Average** €€. **Credit** AmEx, DC, MC, V.

Possibly the oddest culinary experience in Rome: if Fellini had ever directed a James Bond film, he would have set it here. Picture the scene: an obscure order of multi-ethnic

A tiny hole in the wall near the Doria-Pamphili gallery, **La Corte** (via della Gatta 1) is the place to come for smoked salmon and other fishy products such as bottarga (grey mullet roe).

Third World nuns runs a sophisticated French haute cuisine-inspired restaurant in a 16th-century palazzo, with Renaissance frescoes on the ceiling. At 9pm, the diners – many in the ill-fitting brown suits favoured by the international espionage circuit – are interrupted by the tinkle of a silver bell and invited to join in *Ave Maria*. The only disappointment is the food: French classics like quiche lorraine, done with crushing correctness, plus a few daily rotating international specials – couscous on Thursdays. You can dine à la carte or opt for one of four 'menu fisso' meals, at €8.50, €11.50, €15.50 and €26.

Oliphant

Via delle Coppelle 31-2 (06 686 1416). Bus to corso del Rinascimento. **Meals served** 12.30-3pm, 7-11.30pm Mon-Fri, Sun; 7pm-midnight Sat. Closed 1wk Aug. **Average** €€. **Credit** AmEx, DC, MC, V.

Everything's bigger in Texas, as the servings at this Tex-Mex destination attest. This kitchen sends out plates

Le Cornacchie

The best pizzeria

Dar Poeta
See p143.

Remo
See p164.

Al Forno della Soffitta
See p199.

La Pratolina
See p127.

Ciro
See p33.

piled high with nachos, crisp and tangy buffalo wings, and monstrous portions of barbecued pork ribs. Romans think of even Tuscan cuisine as exotic and have little grasp of the Tex-Mex tradition; but these are all pretty decent versions. The usual Mexican favourites are here – tacos, chimichangas, enchiladas, fajitas – along with American staples like burgers and steaks, hot dogs and Caesar salad (which is actually Italo-Mexican in origin, having been invented in Tijuana in 1924 by a man named Caesar Cardini). The bar area is a fun spot for American beers and a mean margarita (if you order for three or more, you get to drink it straight from the pitcher through long straws). Lunch here is less Mexican, more Italian.

Wine bars & pubs

Cul de Sac ★
Piazza Pasquino 73 (06 6880 1094). Bus to corso Vittorio Emanuele (piazza Navona). **Open** noon-4pm, 7pm-12.30am daily. **Credit** AmEx, MC, V.
This is Rome's original wine bar, founded in 1968. It's cramped inside and out, and seating is on communal hostel-style pine benches. But the location – just around the corner from piazza Navona – the decent prices, the friendly ambience and, above all, the huge and regularly updated wine list, keep this place packed. If you manage to secure an outside table, you're in an elite group, and you'll find that you have a ringside view of Pasquino, the most famous of Rome's 'talking statues' – a mutilated ancient marble bust that has served for centuries as an

unofficial peg for satirical poems and political diatribes. Food is standard wine-bar fare, mainly cold: the Greek salad and the lentil soup stand out.

Enoteca del Corso

Corso Vittorio Emanuele 293-95 (06 688 01594).
Bus to corso Vittorio Emanuele (Chiesa Nuova).
Open 10am-9.30pm Mon-Sat. Closed 1wk Aug.
Credit AmEx, DC, MC, V.
Step off the traffic-burdened corso into this cosy little wine bar with a 19th-century feel. Shelves are lined to the ceiling with wines, while chocolates and other gourmet treats are laid out near the bar. Several small tables allow you to sit and eat a cheese and salami plate or the crostini di pâté (bread and pâté nibbles). There are salads too, including a good insalata di rucola e arancio (with rocket and orange). Lunches can be crowded, so go early. For larger groups in the evening, be sure to reserve.

Giulio Passami l'Olio

Via di Monte Giordano 28 (06 688 03 288/www.giulio passamilolio.it). Bus to corso Vittorio Emanuele (Chiesa Nuova). **Open** 6.30pm-4am daily. Closed 1wk Aug.
Credit MC, V.
'Giulio, pass me the oil' is the playful name of this lively, late-opening locale. It's small, candlelit and usually packed with an eclectic crowd of locals. To fill that gap, choose from a selection of salads, meats, cheeses, soups, crêpes and crostini. There are a few adventurous dishes like the wild boar stew with polenta. The menu is filled with wines, grappas, cocktails and plenty of coffees and teas. Wines offered by the glass rotate – today's choices are scribbled on the blackboard by the bar.

Il Bicchiere di Mastai ★

Via dei Banchi Nuovi 52 (06 6819 2228). Bus to
corso Vittorio Emanuele. **Open** 11am-1am Tue-Sun.
Meals served noon-3pm, 7pm-1am Tue-Sun.
Credit AmEx, DC, MC, V.
This new, gourmet wine bar is a charming place for lunch or dinner. The atmosphere is relaxing, the look is country house chic, and the food is ambitious. A selection of enoteca staples – cheese and cured meats – are supplemented by fresh oysters, and serve as the permanent antipasti; the rest of the menu changes weekly. The antipasto of mousse di broccoli con cipolle primaverili e prosciutto d'anatra (Roman broccoli mousse with onions and smoked duck) provides a savoury opening to a meal. The cavatelli pasta with aubergine and pesto sauce was a bit too saucy and underseasoned, but still a competent dish; a carpaccio of mango with a white chocolate mousse was beautifully spare in its presentation, though a tad too sweet. By autumn 2002,

the adjacent palazzo will have opened as a full-time restaurant, leaving this current space to fulfill its enoteca duties with an ample list of wines and distillati.

Il Piccolo

Via del Governo Vecchio 74-5 (06 6880 1746). Bus to corso Vittorio Emanuele. **Open** 11am-3pm, 5pm-2am Mon-Fri; 5pm-2am Sat, Sun. Closed 1wk Aug. **Credit** AmEx, DC, MC, V.

True to its name, this is a tiny place. It's not an unusual size for a wine bar in Italy, however, and the atmosphere is actually quite lively. Tables outside provide additional seating, great for people-watching in this central, hip part of town. The wine list, written out by hand, is a bit difficult to read and not as extensive as you might hope. Still, there's a relatively wide selection of other fermented grape products: wines, ports, dessert wines, grappas. Snacks and sweets are served as well.

La Trinchetta

Via dei Banchi Nuovi 4 (06 6830 0133). Bus to corso Vittorio Emanuele. **Open** 8pm-2am daily. Closed Aug. **Credit** AmEx, MC, V.

This nook is a hidden gem: it's not only an enoteca, it's a grapperia as well, with a huge range of different labels. Owner Enrico Scaduto knows his wines, and is happy to share this knowledge. If you really want to get up to speed on Italian wine culture, enrol for one of the six-week wine-tasting courses here, which will soon be offered in English as well as Italian. To sate the appetite, a selection of cheese and salami are available as well as hot, fresh dishes like lasagna and various torte salate (savoury quiches). La Trinchetta has also begun to theme certain evenings: Thursday, for example, is sushi night, while Ethiopian meals are offered on Sunday. These ethnic soirées should be booked in advance.

Riccioli Café

Piazza delle Coppelle 10A (06 6821 0313). Bus to corso Rinascimento. **Open** 12.30pm-12.30am Mon-Thur, Sun; 12.30pm-1.30am Fri, Sat. **Credit** AmEx, DC, MC, V.

This modern café with neon lighting and upholstered banquettes in marine blue acts as restaurant, sushi bar, tearoom and cocktail lounge. Owned by Massimo Riccioli of La Rosetta fame (*see p61*), it specialises in just-fished seafood. The menu comprises a 'raw bar', sushi and sashimi sections, 'marinati' (ceviche-like marinated seafood) and salads. A dish such as warm potato, octopus and celery salad in a lemon vinaigrette is tasty; but the tuna tartare , though fresh, lacks a certain kick. Prices are a bit steep (particularly for wine) and portions somewhat small; it's better value during the 6-8pm happy hour, when a €7.50 taster menu offers treats like oysters and

Moriondo & Gariglio (via Piè di Marmo 21-22) is chocophile heaven. They specialise in hazelnut gianduiotti, chocolate liqueurs and hollow Valentine hearts, to be filled with diamond rings or similar gewgaws.

Trinity College

tartine (vol-au-vents). Riccioli Café works best, though, as a cocktail bar: this is one of the few places in Rome that makes a decent Cosmopolitan.

Trinity College

Via del Collegio Romano 6 (06 678 6472). Bus to via del Corso/piazza Venezia. **Open** noon-3am daily. **Average** €. **Credit** AmEx, DC, MC, V.
This city-centre pub attracts thirsty tourists and employees of the nearby Ministero dei Beni Culturali (culture ministry) during the day, and all sorts in the evening, when the music gets louder and the scene much livelier. Trinity College has a more authentic feel (though 'tis all blarney) than many of the capital's Irish pubs, and it prides itself on its extensive pub menu. This takes in Mexican specialities such as chicken fajitas (€6.50), various burgers (€8) and a large selection of salads (€6), served in both the low-ceilinged dining room upstairs and the more atmospheric main bar downstairs. There are bacon and egg-based or pasta brunch specials (€13) at weekends to satisfy your egg-cravings.

Bar della Pace

Bars & cafés

Bar del Fico

*Piazza del Fico 26-8 (06 686 5205). Bus to corso Vittorio
Emanuele (Chiesa Nuova).* **Open** 8am-2am daily. Closed
1wk Aug. **No credit cards**.

In the cooler months, this basic bar in the fashionable
hangout zone around via della Pace is no more than a
convenient place to meet before or after a meal. But once
the warmer weather kicks in, the Bar del Fico becomes
the place to be seen. In the evening, particularly at
weekends, the little piazzetta outside – featuring the
venerable fig tree after which it was named – is packed
with beautiful young Romans. Sip a vodka cocktail or a
glass of wine and glare pitilessly at those not fortunate
enough to squeeze in.

Bar della Pace

*Via della Pace 3-7 (06 686 1216). Bus to corso
Rinascimento.* **Open** 3pm-2am Mon; 9am-2am
Tue-Sun. **Credit** MC, V.

Rome's eternally trendy celebrity bar is officially named
L'Antico Caffè della Pace; but everyone refers to it as 'il
Bar'. With its elegant, wood-lined interior, ivy-covered
façade and marble-topped bistro-style tables, it continues
to be a great (though expensive) place from which to
survey passing fashion victims. On summer evenings,
the square overflows with trendy revellers. In the
mornings, tousle-haired locals and expat residents drift
in for a cappuccino and the excellent fresh cornetti.

Caffè Novecento

Via del Governo Vecchio 12 (06 686 5242). Bus to corso Vittorio Emanuele (Chiesa Nuova). **Open** *Sept-Apr* 8.30am-8.30pm Mon-Sat; 3-8.30pm Sun. *May-July* 8.30am-8.30pm Mon-Sat. Closed Aug. **Credit** V.

This charming bistro stands next door to a flower shop. Inside, the mood is feminine and vaguely Parisian, with tables set with lace doilies and an overstuffed antique velvet sofa on which to relax and enjoy a tea, coffee or hot chocolate. A light, quasi-vegetarian buffet is offered at lunchtime (salads, quiches and the like) for an average layout of €10; the selection of freshly made desserts changes daily. Starting in September 2002, dinner will be served in the evening.

Dolce Vita

Piazza Navona 70A (06 6880 6221). Bus to corso Rinascimento. **Open** 8am-midnight daily. **Credit** AmEx, MC, V.

Tiny inside, but with plenty of tables on the square, Dolce Vita is a pleasant alternative to other more touristy bars on the piazza. Great for catching the afternoon sun and watching the endlessly fascinating Navona parade. In summer, you can ogle till 2am. Be warned, though: prices for table service are as steep as anywhere in the square.

La Caffettiera ★

Piazza di Pietra 65 (06 679 8147). Bus to via del Corso. **Open** *Oct-May* 7am-9pm daily. *June-Sept* 7am-9pm Mon-Sat. **Credit** AmEx, DC, MC, V.

This original Roman offshoot of one of Naples' most elegant cafés is always packed in the mornings with politicians and functionaries from nearby parliament buildings and ministries. Collect your cornetto from the glass case by the cash desk and wait patiently for a place at the bar counter, or, if you have time and money to spare, take a seat in the sumptuous tearooms behind. The coffee is excellent, and, among the Neapolitan dolci, the rum baba reigns supreme. Light lunches are also served, and there is a decent selection of malt whiskies. For more, visit its grand cousin, Gran Caffè La Caffettiera (*see p47*).

Pascucci

Via di Torre Argentina 20 (06 686 4816). Bus or tram to largo Argentina. **Open** 6.30am-midnight Mon-Sat. Closed 2wks Aug. **No credit cards**.

This very modest bar in the centre of town has a reputation as milkshake heaven. Milk, though, isn't obligatory: no combination of fresh fruit froth (frullato) is too exotic here, from the classic fragole (strawberry) to the assortito (anything that takes your fancy). In winter, Pascucci's cioccolato con panna (hot chocolate with whipped cream) is a very comforting calorie booster.

Sant'Eustacchio

Piazza di Sant'Eustacchio 82 (06 6880 2048). Bus to corso Rinascimento. **Open** 8.30am-1am Mon-Thur, Sun; 8.30am-1.30am Fri; 8.30am-2am Sat. **No credit cards.**

This may be the most famous coffee bar in the city; its walls are plastered with celebrity testimonials. The coffee is quite extraordinary – if very expensive. The Gran Caffè is served in a large cup and made to a secret recipe (hence the screens around the large coffee machines): the schiuma (froth) is part of the experience, and should be sipped demurely with a spoon. Unless you specify caffè 'amaro', it comes heavily sugared. The granita and parfaits di caffè are heavenly.

Tazza d'Oro

Via degli Orfani 84 (06 678 9792). Bus to via del Corso (largo Chigi). **Open** 7am-8pm Mon-Sat. Closed 1wk Aug. **Credit** AmEx, DC, MC, V.

The powerful aroma wafting from this ancient torrefazione (coffee toastery) overlooking the Pantheon is a siren call to coffee lovers. Follow your nose, and you won't regret the trip. Inside, the shop is packed with coffee sacks and kitsch posters showing leggy Brazilian coffee-pickers working in the sun. Both tourists and local regulars flock here for the excellent, cut-price granita di caffè (coffee sorbet), which is served with cream (con panna) or without (senza panna). There's freshly ground coffee, and in winter this place offers a mean cioccolata calda con panna (hot chocolate with whipped cream) that will take the chill right out of your bones.

Sant'Eustacchio

Fiori & Ghetto

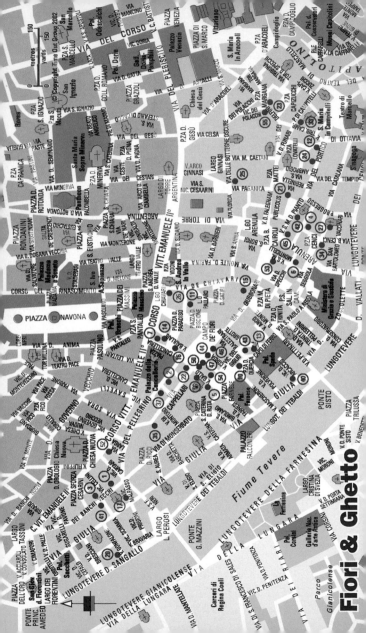

The southern part of the warren of streets that forms the core of the Centro Storico still has a real neighbourhood feel. Stellar rents have not dragged it too far upmarket, so antique shops and chic cafés stand cheek by jowl with dingy motorcycle repair shops and furniture restorers. The beating heart of the area is the square of Campo de'Fiori, with its picturesque morning market and fringe of pavement bars. On summer evenings, a seething mass crowds in here to swap ciaos and down a glass or three. To the south of the Campo, elegant piazza Farnese and via Giulia keep their aristocratic distance from the rabble. Further east, on the other side of via Arenula, stands the Ghetto, a tiny area of medieval lanes that is still the hub of Rome's long-standing Jewish community.

Restaurants

Albistrò

Via dei Banchi Vecchi 140A (06 686 5274). Bus to corso Vittorio Emanuele (Chiesa Nuova) or Ponte Mazzini. **Meals served** 7.30-11pm Mon, Tue, Thur Sat; 12.30-3pm, 7.30-11pm Sun. Closed mid July-mid Aug. **Average** €€. **Credit** AmEx, DC, MC, V.

The Swiss owner has carved a bistro ambience into this narrow space, which extends out the back into a pretty courtyard, where tables are laid out in the summer, neighbours permitting. The menu is strong on soups, quiches and salads, though there are also a few pasta dishes and risottos. The kitchen is variable at best; a filetto di spigola con salsa di finocchi e patate novelle (sea bass with fennel sauce and new potatoes) looked and tasted tired, and the potatoes were shrivelled and clearly reheated. Best to stick to the simpler platters and order a decent bottle from the limited but well-priced list. Mein host is quite a character, and pleasant enough once you get used to his gruff exterior. The clientele tends to be international, with a strong presence of UN lifers from the FAO. From 6pm to 7.30pm on Thursday, Friday and Saturday, Albistrò operates as a wine bar, with a selection of Spanish-style tapas.

Campo de'Fiori market. *See p81.*

Al Bric

Via del Pellegrino 51-2 (06 687 9533). Bus to corso Vittorio Emanuele (piazza della Cancelleria). **Meals served** *Sept-June* 7.30-11.30pm Tue-Sun. *July, Aug* 7.30-11.30pm Tue-Sun. **Average** €€€. **Credit** DC, MC, V. This wine-oriented restaurant not far from campo de' Fiori is notable for its extensive selection of cheeses and its entrance bottle room. There is a certain preciousness about the walls lined with deconstructed wine crates, the intimate tables, the soft lighting and, above all, the nouvelle cuisine portions. Some of the kitchen's creative Italian offerings work well, like the pappardelle tirate a mano con lepre e salsiccia (handmade flat pasta with a wild hare and sausage sauce); and it does an inventive take on beef stroganoff. But many dishes fall well short of even the most basic expectations. Take, for instance, the 'crunchy scallops', which consists of a grand total of three scallops, overcooked and unpleasantly fishy.

Service is equally minimalist; unfortunately, the bill is not. And the ritual whereby one is forced to get up and choose one's wine in the lobby could easily be replaced with an ingenious portable document that has met with much favour elsewhere: a wine list.

Al Ciabot

Via dei Banchi Vecchi 129-31 (06 6880 9595). Bus to corso Vittorio Emanuele (Chiesa Nuova). **Meals served** *Mid Sept-June* 7.30-11.30pm Tue-Sat; 12.30-2.30pm, 7.30-11.30pm Sun. *July-mid Sept* 7.30-11.30pm Tue-Sun. Closed Aug. **Average** €€€. **Credit** DC, MC, V.

Al Ciabot is similar in decor and approach to its parent restaurant, Al Bric, with simple wooden tables, colourful ceramic plates, with a tantalising selection of French and Italian cheeses in the window. But the formula (like the kitchen) seems to work better here, though many of the same dishes are present, such as orzo perlato al reblochon di savoia (pearl barley risotto-style in a reblochon cheese sauce). If you're not up to a full three-course meal, you can always opt for a selection from the cheese board. As in Al Bric, you have to go through the faintly irritating ritual of getting up from your table to study the wine list and bottles in the back room; beware of pointing at random, as prices range from €15 to over €300 per bottle, and your bill can suddenly double.

Al Pompiere

Via Santa Maria dei Calderari 38 (06 686 8377). Bus/tram to via Arenula. **Meals served** 12.30-3pm, 7.30-11pm Mon-Sat. Closed mid July-Aug. **Average** €€€. **Credit** AmEx, MC, V.

Occupying the first floor of historic Palazzo Cenci-Bolognetti, the frescoed, high-ceilinged rooms of 'The Fireman' offer a spacious, elegant but not overpriced alternative to many of its more cramped Ghetto rivals; though service (prompted, perhaps, by the surroundings) can be a little arrogant. The menu is based on solid Roman fare with some very unusual touches. The more standard dishes include such as coda alla vaccinara (braised oxtail and celery), deep-fried Roman Jewish specialities, from carciofi alla giudia (artichokes cooked until they resemble crisp sunflowers) and frittura alla pecorara (fried ricotta, artichokes, lamb chop and brains). Along with these, though, are a few ancient Roman dishes, such as spezzatino al cedro (beef stew with citron), said to be from an recipe that Tiberius' cook Apicius allegedly created for the emperor at his holiday home on Capri. The long arm of the fritto extends to the speciality dessert, crema fritta (deep-fried custard). The wine list is decent enough, and a special mention must go to the English translation of the menu. Anyone for 'wrinkled salad' with 'frost fish'?

Another good Campo takeaway option, **Panino Giusto** (Campo de' Fiori 55) does a good range of filled rolls and salads, to be eaten in or taken away.

Fiori & Ghetto

Ar Galletto

Vicolo del Gallo 1 (06 686 1714). Bus to corso Vittorio Emanuele (piazza della Cancelleria). **Meals served** 12.15-3pm, 7.30-11.15pm Mon-Sat. Closed 10 days Aug. **Average** €€. **Credit** AmEx, DC, MC, V.

You don't need to pay the inflated prices charged by Camponeschi (*see below*) for a ringside view of piazza Farnese. Ar Galletto, a far humbler trattoria, has tables on the square in summer. The food is standard Roman, but dishes like penne all'arrabbiata or spaghetti alle vongole are appetising and – for the location – well priced. Service is brisk but friendly.

Bruschetteria degli Angeli

Piazza B Cairoli 2A (06 6880 5789). Bus/tram to via Arenula. **Meals served** 12.30-3pm, 7.30pm-1am Mon-Sat; 7.30pm-1am Sun. **Average** €. **Credit** AmEx, DC, MC, V.

This unpretentious, pub-like diner overlooks a dusty park, set just back from tram-bound via Arenula. As the name suggests, the star turns are bruschette – thick toasted bread, here in mega format, with various toppings, from radicchio e pancetta (red chicory and bacon) to zucchine grigliate e mozzarella di bufala (grilled courgettes and buffalo mozzarella); prices vary from €6.70 to €8.80. There are also pasta dishes, grilled steaks, and a good range of draught beers, including Leffe double malt. On Wednesday and Thursday evenings there's live music and food with a Spanish or Cuban slant.

Campo

Piazza della Cancelleria 64 (06 683 01162). Bus to via del Corso (piazza della Cancelleria). **Meals served** 8pm-midnight daily. Closed 1wk Aug. **Average** €€€. **Credit** AmEx, DC, MC, V.

Although the name refers to nearby campo de' Fiori, this consciously urbane restaurant – the first in Rome to be designed along Feng Shui lines – couldn't be further in style from the populist hubbub of the square. Climb a sleek, steep staircase to the second floor dining area with sparse decor and painfully trendy waiting staff; large windows allow you to observe the the hoi polloi below. Campo specialises in fresh Mediterranean fish such as carpaccio di spigola (thin slices of raw sea bass); sushi and sashimi are available most days. If you yearn for the London or New York scene, Campo is worth shelling out on. Otherwise, it's probably better to ignore its hipper-than-thou air and exercise your credit card elsewhere.

Camponeschi

Piazza Farnese 50A (06 687 4927). Bus/tram to largo Argentina or bus to Ponte Sisto. **Meals served** 7.30pm-12.30am Mon-Sat. Closed 1wk Aug. **Average** €€€€€. **Credit** AmEx, DC, MC, V.

Right on the Campo, **Da Giovanni** (Campo de' Fiori 39) does the best takeway pizza in the area – try the fiori di zucca, which is topped with mozzarella and courgette flowers.

One of Rome's most elegant and expensive restaurants sits regally on one of its most photogenic squares, piazza Farnese. Elaborate flower arrangements and an affable maître d' greet you as you arrive, and large gilded mirrors allow you to check that you're looking suitably suave. On some evenings, a jazz band warbles discreetly in the corner; in warmer weather you can sit outside and admire the newly restored façade of Michelangelo's palazzo, now the home of the French Embassy. The food is equally polished. Antipasti include foie gras al porto con uva candita (foie gras in port with candied grapes). A primo such as risotto con ostriche belon e champagne (risotto with Belon oysters and champagne) might be followed by a secondo of gamberi al vermouth con riso pilaff (shrimp cooked in vermouth with rice pilaff). But it's all

Campo

rather showy in its flaunting of ingredients like oysters and champagne, and the stratospheric prices (around €90 per head for a three-course meal and a modest bottle of wine) are not warranted by the play-safe cuisine. At Camponeschi you're not paying for culinary excellence so much as a name, a location and the warm glow of privilege. Still, lots of people are prepared to do just that – so if you come, reserve well ahead of time.

Costanza

Piazza del Paradiso 63-5 (06 686 1717). Bus to via del Corso (Sant'Andrea della Valle). **Meals served** 12.30-3pm, 7.30-11.30pm Mon-Sat. Closed 3wks Aug. **Average** €€€€. **Credit** AmEx, DC, MC, V.

This is the kind of place your father might bring you to, in order to regale you with stories of what he got up to in Rome in the 1960s. Costanza has been around for years, but the premises have been around for even longer: the restaurant is built into the arches under the Teatro di Pompeo, which dates back to 60BC. Service is brisk but indulgent; the cuisine is based on the kind of well-executed pan-Italian comfort food that brought your father here all those years ago. Don't miss the antipasti fritti – a fill-you-up-before-you-starter that includes deep-fried mozzarella, fiori di zucca (courgette flowers), supplì (rice balls) and crocchette di patate (mashed potato balls). The Roman Jewish tradition of the nearby Ghetto is present in the house speciality, carciofi all guidia (deep-fried artichokes). Tasty pasta dishes include tagliolini ai moscardini con bottarga (long pasta strips with baby squid and fish roe) and the tegamino di gnocchi (spinach gnocchi baked in a tomato and cheese casserole).

Da Giggetto

Via Portico d'Ottavia 21-2 (06 686 1105). Bus to Isola Tiberina or bus/tram to via Arenula. **Meals served** 12.30-3pm, 7.30-11pm Tue-Sun. Closed 2wks July-Aug. **Average** €€. **Credit** AmEx, DC, MC, V.

This old standby in the Jewish Ghetto gets a mention in just about every tourist guide, and there's a good reason for it. A troop of old-fashioned waiters serves up decent versions of classics of cucina ebraica like carciofi alla giudia (fried whole artichoke flowers), melanzane alla parmigiana (aubergine with parmesan gratin) and fried baccalà (salt cod). The atmosphere is warm and bustling, with large tables of tourists – both Italian and foreign – enjoying the ambience and the plentiful helpings. A bonus is the unexpectedly extensive winelist, with reasonable mark-ups. In warm weather, outside tables have a view of first-century Portico d'Ottavia, once the entrance to a huge colonnaded square, now part of a new open-to-view archaeological area.

Da Sergio ★

Vicolo delle Grotte 27 (06 686 4293). Bus/tram to via Arenula or bus to Ponte Sisto. **Meals served** 12.30-3.30pm, 6.30pm-midnight Mon-Sat. Closed 2wks Aug. **Average** €€. **Credit** DC, MC, V.

It's cheap, it's friendly, it does good home cooking and it's always full of locals. Add a central location near Campo de' Fiori and honest-to-goodness trattoria ambience, and it's not hard to understand why there's often a queue outside. The red and white checked paper tablecloths blend perfectly with the hot chillis hanging from the ceiling, the boar's head on the wall and the framed covers of 1950s film magazines. The pasta portions are huge (you can order halves) and the beef (kept in a glassed-in fridge near the entrance) is top quality. The day's bill of fare is generally recited out loud, but if you want a chuckle, ask for the few copies of the menus kept for tourists and admire their translations. Da Sergio does great versions of bucatini all'amatriciana (thick, hollow spaghetti with a bacon, tomato and pecorino sauce) and penne all'arrabbiata (billed as 'pasta with tomato souce hotchill'). Among the secondi, the

Costanza. *See p87.*

straccetti stand out (the 'nocket salad' these thin strips of beef are served with is, of course, rughetta, or rocket). The delicious bread here comes from a good local bakery, as do most of the desserts.

Ditirambo

Piazza della Cancelleria 74 (06 687 1626). Bus to corso Vittorio Emanuele (piazza della Cancelleria). **Meals served** 8-11.30pm Mon; 1-3pm, 8-11.30pm Tue-Sun. Closed Aug. **Average** €€. **Credit** MC, V.

This funky trattoria around the corner from campo de' Fiori has good-value food based on fresh, mainly organic ingredients. It is traditional fare with a creative kick, as in the malfatti ai fiori di zucca (pasta with courgette flowers) and the pici al ragu di cinghiale (Tuscan spaghetti with wild boar sauce). Meaty secondi include the fillet steak with balsamic vinegar, or the tagliata di manzo in salsa di timo (sliced beef steak with thyme). The kitchen always seems to be out of roast potatoes, so go for the polpette di melanzane alla calabrese (Calabrian aubergine fritters). It's regularly booked up in the evenings, despite the occasionally brusque service.

Filetti di Baccalà

Largo Librai 88 (06 686 4018). Bus/tram to via Arenula.
Meals served 5.30-11.15pm Mon-Sat. Closed Aug, 1wk
Dec-Jan. **Average** €. **No credit cards.**
Officially known as Dar Filettaro a Santa Barbara,
habitués of this place take their cue from the sign over
the door, which promises exactly what you get – salt cod
fillets in batter. Alongside the obligatory filetti there are
other goodies such as fried courgettes. Service is brisk,
the ambience spit and sawdust, but it's in a pretty square,
it's dead cheap, and it's one of the few places in Rome that
allows people who choose to do so to eat dinner (the
horror! the horror!) as early as 6pm.

Grappolo d'Oro

*Piazza della Cancelleria 80 (06 689 7080). Bus to corso
Vittorio Emanuele (piazza della Cancelleria).* **Meals
served** 7.30-11pm Mon; 12.30-2.30pm, 7.30-11pm Tue-
Sun. Closed Aug. **Average** €€. **Credit** AmEx, MC, V.
This bright, sunny trattoria, just across the way from its
sister, Ditirambo (*see p89*), is a tad more traditional and
sophisticated. Both kitchens share the same culinary
aesthetic – and even the same ladies who make pasta by
hand every afternoon between meals – serving a
sampling of fresh, simple trattoria dishes from the
different regions of Italy. In the 'Grapes of gold' you can
start with the insalata di polipo verace con carciofi
(octopus salad with artichokes) before moving on to a
well-balanced version of rigatoni all'amatriciana (pasta
in a tomato, bacon and pecorino sauce). The spezzatino
di vitello con puré di carote (veal stew with a carrot purée)
is a good, meaty winter option, although there is also a
wide range of fresh fish and seafood. As a contorno (side
dish), try the spinaci saltati con pinoli e uvetta (sautéd
spinach with pine nuts and raisins), a classic southern
Italian flavour combo that, believe it or not, makes you
wonder, 'Why didn't I think of this?'

Il Drappo

*Vicolo del Malpasso 9 (06 687 7365). Bus to corso
Vittorio Emanuele (Chiesa Nuova) or Ponte Mazzini.*
Meals served 7-11pm Mon-Sat. Closed 3wks Aug.
Average €€€. **Credit** AmEx, DC, MC, V.
This pretty restaurant on a leafy side street just off via
Giulia has been serving Sardinian specialities since 1974.
The ceiling is covered with the drapes that give the place
its name: elaborate cloths designed to cover the statues
carried through Sardinian towns on saint days. The menu
is a reflection of the island itself, split between abundant
seafood and the more rustic, meat-based cooking of the
interior. Tuck into the light, crispy carta di musica (a sort
of Sardinian popadom) while awaiting a pasta dish like
spaghetti with spiny lobster sauce. One of the trademark

dishes is the porchetta al mirto (myrtle-scented roast baby pig), which is moist and flavourful. A special of lamb prepared the same way, however, was extremely fatty, while the rombo al forno con patate (oven-baked turbot with potatoes) was decent, but nothing special. The lesson: stick with time-tested Sardinian menu standards. Finish up with seadas, a Sardinian sheep's milk cheese served fried and covered in warm honey.

Il Gonfalone ★

Via del Gonfalone 7 (06 6880 1269). Bus to Ponte Mazzini or corso Vittorio Emanuele (Chiesa Nuova). **Meals served** 7.45-11pm Tue-Fri; 12.30-2.45pm, 7.45-11pm Sat, Sun. Closed 2wks Aug. **Credit** AmEx, DC, MC, V.

It hasn't been open long, but this reasonably priced creative Italian restaurant housed in a Renaissance palazzo just off via Giulia has already made a name for itself. Chilean chef Victor Hugo (yes, that's his real name) changes the menu every two weeks according to what the market offers. So you're unlikely to find the cavatelli mantecati con pesce spada, uvetta e pinoli (pasta with swordfish, sultanas and pine nuts) or the antipasto of bresaola (thinly sliced dried beef) with pink grapefruit in a honey vinaigrette that we enjoyed on our visit, but whatever is on offer should be good. The pretty interior can seem a bit cramped; in summer, the little piazza outside is a charming place for an al fresco meal. A well-chosen wine list is overseen by one of the owners of the Cavour 313 wine bar (*see p186*). On a good night, Il Gonfalone offers a really good value gourmet dining experience: so be sure to book ahead.

La Carbonara

Campo de' Fiori 23 (06 686 4783). Bus to corso Vittorio Emanuele (piazza della Cancelleria). **Meals served** 12.30-3pm, 7.30-11pm Mon, Wed-Sun. Closed 3wks Aug. **Average** €€. **Credit** AmEx, MC, V.

At one end of Rome's most photogenic square, this place looks like a tourist trap. In fact, this old trooper does surprisingly honest cucina romana, with traditional favourites like the spaghetti alla carbonara from which its name derives. The wine list and desserts are uninspired, but it's the setting that counts here. Remember where you are, though, and keep an eye on your bag at outside tables.

In a lane connecting the Campo with piazza Farnese, **Le Piramidi** (vicolo del Gallo 11) does some of the best falafel in pitta bread this side of Cairo.

La Taverna degli Amici

Piazza Margana 36 (06 6992 0637). Bus to piazza Venezia. **Open** 12.30-3pm, 7.30pm-midnight Mon-Thur, Sun. Closed 10 days Aug. **Average** €€€. **Credit** AmEx, DC, MC, V.

The setting here is idyllic, in an ivy-draped square on the Ghetto side of piazza Venezia. Over the years, the creative Roman cooking has had its ups and downs; our last visit

8

La Taverna del Ghetto

KOSHER
- JEWISH ARTICHOKE
- CHICKEN LIVER PATÉ
- ARTICHOKES SALAD WITH LEMON
- LASAGNA OF THE DAY
- RAVIOL
- LAMB
- FRIED
- SEA 30

CUCINA EBRAICA ROMANESCA

KOSH
7W3
JEWISH ARTI
CARCIOFO ALL
TORTINO DI ALK
CONCIA DI ZU
PUNTARELLE IN X
FRITTO DI FIORI
FRITTO DI CERVE
FETTUCCINE AL
TAGLIATELLE CON LE
BACCALA ALLA X
POLPETTE DI X
CICORIA CON X
ABBACCHIO ALLA

La Taverna del Ghetto

registered an upswing, with a good risotto of radicchio and pine nuts followed by a textbook filetto di manzo (beef fillet) with shallots. Though meaty Roman classics are not lacking, there are also a number of vegetarian options to be found here. Service is friendly, the wine list short but adequate. Understandably, the outside tables are much sought after.

La Taverna del Ghetto

Via Portico d'Ottavia 7B (06 6880 9771). Bus to Isola Tiberina or bus/tram to via Arenula. **Meals served** noon-3pm, 7-11pm Sun-Thur; noon-3pm Fri; 7-11pm Sat. **Average** €€. **Credit** AmEx, MC, V.

Until the debut of Yotvata (*see p98*), this was the only truly kosher Jewish restaurant in the Ghetto. It does recognisable Roman cucina ebraica, but is neither particularly memorable nor particularly cheap. Behind a touristy façade on the main Ghetto street lie a series of simple vaulted rooms with exposed bricks and a faintly musty air. Here old-style, attentive waiters serve up classics like carciofi alla giudia (deep-fried artichokes) and aliciotti e indivia (anchovies and endives). Pasta courses are more creative but not always successful: a taglitatelle con cernia e fiori di zucca (with sea bass and courgette flowers) came with cherry tomatoes in place of the flowers. And the sauce drowning the classic Roman spring salad, puntarelle con le alici (chicory tips), was far too vinegary. Still, the wine list is intriguing, with a range of kosher Italian and Israeli wines at reasonable prices.

Le Bain ★

Via delle Botteghe Oscure 32-3 (06 686 5673). Bus/tram to largo Argentina. **Meals served** 8pm-midnight Tue-Sat; 12.30-3.30pm Sun. *Bar* 7pm-2am Tue-Sat; 6-9pm Sun. Closed Aug. **Average** €€€. **Credit** AmEx, DC, MC, V.

One of a new generation of urban-chic locales, this restaurant and lounge is a hybrid born from the grafting of serious kitchen staff on to what was, briefly, one of Rome's trendiest nightclubs. The young chef cut his teeth on the Amalfi Coast under a Michelin-starred boss; his mostly southern Italian preparations are enlivened by fusion influences and presented with nouvelle delicacy – and in nouvelle portions. The antipasto of tiger prawns wrapped in bacon on soft polenta and broccoli with sausage ragù has plenty of character, but the risotto mantecato al radicchio rosso e fonduta di asiago (risotto with radicchio and melted asiago cheese) is prepared with what appears to be Thai jasmine rice – which lacks the characteristic al dente bite of Italian risotto rice. Still, the seabass fillet with thyme, sautéed spinach, and a sour fig sauce is delicious, and beautifully presented. The same goes for the cassata nuda, a ricotta-rich cross between two Sicilian staple sweets, the cassata and the cannolo. Prices are a bit steep: clearly, the cost of the interior decoration and the PR are being passed on to the customer. Still, Le Bain has more culinary assurance and sexy ambience than most places in Rome can offer.

L'Insalata Ricca

Largo dei Chiavari 85 (06 6880 3656). Bus to corso Vittorio Emanuele (Sant'Andrea della Valle).
Meals served noon-3.30pm, 6.30-11.30pm daily.
Average €. **Credit** AmEx, DC, MC, V.
L'Insalata Ricca is a good answer to that classic Roman dilemma – where to go when you're dying for a decent salad. In addition, although it's not exclusively vegetarian, it's still a reasonably safe haven for veggies. Another Rome rarity. The Italian/English menu lists over 30 different insalate, from baires (walnuts, apple and melted gorgonzola) to speck (with speck ham, fontina cheese and croutons). The bruschette provide a suitably filling starter, especially those topped with marinated aubergine or robiola cheese and sesame seeds. Over the past few years, the success of L'Insalata Ricca has led not only to its own expansion but to the opening of a rash of lookalikes scattered around the city, but the mothership remains the best. It even has ample outdoor seating in the summer months, so you can have your salad al fresco. Arrive early if you want your place in the sun.

Piperno

Monte de' Cenci 9 (06 6880 6629). Bus to Isola Tiberina or bus/tram to via Arenula. **Meals served** 12.45-2.15pm, 8-10.15pm Tue-Sat; 12.45-2.15pm Sun. Closed Aug, Easter, 1wk Christmas. **Average** €€€€. **Credit** DC, MC, V.
Hidden in the heart of the Jewish Ghetto, this ultra-traditional stalwart of the Roman dining scene is the temple of the perfect carciofo alla giudia (deep-fried artichoke) – crisp outside and tender within. Other cucina ebraica specialities you'll find here are the excellent fritto vegetariano – though it's a typically loose Italian definition of 'vegetarian', as besides delicate fried courgette flowers and mini-mozzarellas it includes salt cod fillets. Among the meaty secondi is a good, though rather heavy, animelle con i carciofi (lamb entrails with artichokes). Whether you eat on the ancient piazzetta or in the formal but far from stuffy dining room, this venerable restaurant with its affable, white-jacketed waiters takes you back to a leisurely age when meals were long, urbane and sociable. You'll need to socialise for a bit after round one in order to make room for the speciality dessert, palle del nonno (grandpa's balls): calorific bignès filled with ricotta and chocolate.

The branch of **L'Insalata Ricca** at piazza di Pasquino 72 (06 6830 7881) is the only bona fide Centro Storico offshoot of this famed salad centre.

San Teodoro

Via dei Fienili 49-51 (06 678 0933). Bus to via Petroselli. **Meals served** 12.30-3.30pm, 7.30-12.30pm Mon-Sat. Closed mid Jan-mid Feb. **Average** €€€.
Credit AmEx, DC, MC, V.

At the time of going to press, this restaurant in a charming residential enclave in the shadow of the Palatine was still closed for major refurbishment. Before the shutdown, it was a great place for an al fresco meal with decently cooked seafood and a small but well-selected wine list. We await developments with interest, and trust that the makeover will not be taken as a pretext to hike up the prices, which had already begun to move away from the good-value zone.

Sora Lella

Via Ponte Quattro Capi 16 (06 686 1601). Bus to Isola Tiberina. **Meals served** 12.50-2.30pm, 7.50-10.45pm Mon-Sat. Closed Aug. **Average** €€€€.
Credit AmEx, DC, MC, V.

Sora Lella was the plump, homely sister of even plumper Roman film character actor Aldo Fabrizi. A sort of Roman celebrity Queen Mum, she became a folk idol and a TV star in her own right. Her son set up this upmarket Roman trattoria on the Tiber island in her honour after she died in 1993. It avoids the obvious trap of folksy kitsch, and offers good, modernised Roman cooking, with filling classics such as pasta e patate (pasta and potatoes) or gnocchi all'amatriciana playing off against more creative options like paccheri al sugo di pesce (pasta in fish sauce) or filetto al Cesanese del Piglio (beef fillet in a sauce made from a red Lazio wine). Some dishes fail to reach the peaks, and prices are a little high for what you get, but the ambience is warm and welcoming, service efficient and the wine list well stocked.

Vecchia Roma

Piazza Campitelli 18 (06 686 4604). Bus to via del Teatro di Marcello. **Meals served** 12.30-3pm, 7.30-11pm Mon, Tue, Thur-Sun. Closed 3wks Aug. **Average** €€€€.
Credit AmEx, DC, MC, V.

Without its setting, this restaurant would not really make the grade – but what a setting it is. Piazza Campitelli, on the edge of the Ghetto, has to be one of the nicest places in Rome to sit outside. Brothers Tonino and Giuseppe (the latter is one of the pioneers of post-war Italian restaurants in London) do a series of tried, tested and occasionally tired versions of Italian classics. Among the primi the pandacce (freshly made pasta) with fresh pecorino cheese and broccoli stand out. The winter menu is dominated by an exhaustive series of variations on polenta sauces, grandly entitled 'fantasie di polenta', while the summer

Fiori & Ghetto

Historic cucina ebraica

Rome is forever bound to its Catholic history, but this very religious city is also home to the oldest surviving diasporic Jewish community in the world.

With a foundation dating back to the second century BC, the Jewish community in Rome has a cultural tradition spanning millennia with roots that are predominantly Sephardic (deriving from Spanish and Portuguese Jews who fled after the 1492 Inquisition).

These Sephardim brought to Italy the New World ingredients that their Iberian explorers had discovered: tomatoes, peppers, corn, potatoes and pumpkin. They also brought elements of Arab-influenced Iberian cuisine to Italy, which explains the large number of cucina ebraica dishes featuring raisins and pine nuts, as well as the penchant for sweet-and-sour sauces.

Since the Roman Jews have historically been fairly orthodox and observant, many recipes derive from the necessity of keeping kosher. No pork, game or rabbit are to be found in Jewish recipes, just as no shellfish or fish without scales can be served in a kosher home. So meat dishes contain

only kosher beef or chicken, and cannot be mixed with dairy products. The necessity of scaled fish explains the popularity of baccalà (salt cod) in traditional Jewish Roman cooking. It's served every way imaginable: fried, mixed with oil to form a spreadable paste or stewed with tomatoes.

Rabbinic law prohibits Jews from doing any form of manual labour (including cooking) on the Sabbath, thus many dishes are served hot on Friday night and at room temperature on Saturday – a practice that gave rise to a repertoire of tasty leftovers.

A large part of the Roman Jewish diet is comprised of vegetables. Most dishes containing fennel or aubergine, for example, are of Jewish origin, as Catholic Italians originally shunned these exotic vegetables.

The same holds true for the ubiquitous Roman artichoke. Carciofi alla giudia (literally, 'Jewish-style' artichokes) are simply whole, deep-fried artichoke flowers, cooked until tender inside. In a way, they represent Roman cucina ebraica at its finest: fresh ingredients, simply prepared, and rooted in tradition.

menu is shaped around a vast selection of salads, each one with a different woman's name. But the service is uncommonly fine, the wines are excellent, and, well… this would be the perfect place to bring your parents, basically. As long as they're paying.

Yotvata

Piazza Cenci 70 (06 6813 4481). Bus/tram to via Arenula. **Meals served** noon-3pm, 7.30-11pm Mon-Thur, Sun; noon-3pm Fri; 7.30-11pm Sat. Closed Jewish holidays. **Average** €-€€. **No credit cards.**

This restaurant in the Jewish ghetto is named after a place near Eilat, Israel, mentioned in the Bible as 'the land where the water flows.' The menu is kosher dairy, which means that no meat can be served, although kosher fish (that is, those that have scales) is plentiful. Antipasti consist of a range of bruschette and crostini as well as a selection of fried dishes, including the traditional carciofo alla giudia (fried whole artichoke). The spaghetti al ragu di pesce (with tomato and fish sauce) has just enough sauce. The menu includes a variety of pizzas, fish second courses, and lots of vegetable contorni.

Pizzerie

Acchiappafantasmi

Via dei Cappellari 66 (06 687 3462). Bus to corso Vittorio Emanuele (Chiesa Nuova). **Meals served** *Oct-May* noon-2.30pm, 7.30pm-midnight Mon, Wed-Sun. *June-Sept* 7.30pm-midnight daily. Closed 1wk Aug. **Average** €€. **Credit** AmEx, DC, MC, V.

The tongue-twisting name translates as 'Ghostbusters', a handle justified by the Commisso brothers' prize-winning product: a spook-shaped mozzarella, cherry tomato and oregano pizza, with olives for eyes. But there are also Calabrian treats like 'nduja (a paste to spread on rustic bread, made with sausage and peppers) and bocconcini golosi (mozzarella wrapped in bacon). These can be sampled as part of a reasonably priced range of taster menus (€13-€19). Try the aubergine parmigiana, here with the interesting addition of ham and hard-boiled eggs, and the spinach salad (with bacon, fresh mushrooms, walnuts and parmesan). Be sure to leave room for dessert, as the gelato, brought in from the Calabrian town of Pizzo Calabro, is considered by many to be the best in Italy.

International

Sciam ★

Via del Pellegrino 56 (06 6830 8957). Bus to corso Vittorio Emanuele (Chiesa Nuova). **Meals served** 12.30pm-2am daily. **Average** €. **Credit** AmEx, MC, V.

Rome's only kosher takeaway pizza outlet, **Zi' Fenizia** (via Santa Maria del Pianto 64) has over 40 flavours, including aliciotti e indivia (anchovy and endives).

Fiori & Ghetto

This is one of Rome's more unusual bar/restaurants. On one side is a shop that restores Persian rugs and sells Middle Eastern glass tableware and baubles, which are piled up in crates in an extraordinary warren of Roman and medieval cellars down below: ask the owner, Youssef Hallek, if you can have a look around. On the other side is a spectacular Ottoman café, with its series of long rooms with bare, Roman brick walls adorned with maiolica-tiled fountains, low walnut furniture inlaid with mother of pearl, wooden ceiling panels in geometric patterns and clusters of colourful grape lights. It feels like you've left 21st-century Rome and stumbled into 19th-century Constantinople. The food is simple mezze fare: tabouleh, houmous, ful damasco (fava beans with olive oil, lemon, tomato and parsley) and other Syrian classics – all entirely vegetarian. They average €3.10 a portion, but you get six for the price of five. There's no alcohol – have a mint tea or mango juice instead. Or if you really want to get in the mood, order a narghile (hubble-bubble pipe) – €5.15 for two people – and commandeer the backgammon board.

Thien Kim

Via Giulia 201 (06 6830 7832). Bus to Ponte Sisto.
Meals served 8-11.30pm Mon-Sat. Closed Aug.
Average €€. **Credit** AmEx, DC, MC, V.
When this Vietnamese place opened in 1975, coming here was more a political statement than a culinary choice. But it has survived into more blasé times, and the offerings are reasonably authentic and generally tasty. Starters include spring rolls and zuppa agro-piccante (sour and spicy soup). Recommended main dishes include the costoletta di maiale in salsa dolce (tiny pork ribs in an Asian barbecue sauce), anatra in salsa piccante (duck in 'hot' sauce – although in ours there was nary a trace of chilli), and pollo in salsa saté e citronella (chicken in a satay-lemongrass sauce). There is also a large selection of frogs' legs dishes, if you're into the little jumpers.

Wine bars & pubs

Il Goccetto ★

Via dei Banchi Vecchi, 14 (06 686 4268). Bus to corso Vittorio Emanuele (Chiesa Nuova)/Ponte Mazzini.
Open 11.30am-2pm, 5.30-11pm Mon-Sat. Closed 3wks Aug. **Credit** AmEx, MC, V.
One of the more serious Centro Storico wine bars, occupying part of a medieval bishop's house with original painted ceilings, Sergio Ceccarelli's long-running enoteca is a bit like a Roman version of a Soho pub, with a cast

of artsy regulars propping up the bar. Wine is the main point, with a satisfying and ever-changing range of by-the-glass options, but there's a good selection of whiskies and distillati here too, as well as a small but impressive cheese and salami board.

La Bottega del Vino da Anacleto Bleve

Via Santa Maria del Pianto 9-11 (06 686 5970).
Bus/tram to via Arenula. **Open** *Enoteca* 8am-8pm Mon-Sat. *Meals served* 12.45-3pm Mon-Sat. Closed 3wks Aug.
Average €-€€. **Credit** AmEx, DC, MC, V.
This historic wine shop's carefully selected range of bottles by top Italian producers ensures that La Bottega is well patronised by locals, though increasing space has gradually been given over to tables and a lunch clientele of business folk and expats. The food is fresh and simple, with mixed salads, plates of formaggi misti (mixed cheeses) or salami and carpaccio, plus one or two daily specials. Ordering usually takes place at the counter, so what you see is literally what you get. The wine by the glass menu is select, but prices can be a tad steep compared to other venues. Arrive early or be prepared for the inevitable queue.

L'Angolo Divino

Via dei Balestrari 12 (06 686 4413). Bus or tram to largo Argentina. **Open** *mid Sept-mid Apr* 10am-2.30pm Mon; 10am-2.30pm, 5.30pm-1am Tue-Sun. *Mid Apr-mid Sept* 10am-2.30pm Mon; 10am-2.30pm, 5.30pm-1am Tue-Sat; 5.30pm-1am Sun. Closed 1wk Aug. **Average** €.
Credit MC, V.

Fiori & Ghetto

This punningly named bar on a quiet street near campo de' Fiori has come up in the world since it opened as a humble vini e oli 50 years ago. Over 20 reds, whites and dessert wines are available by the glass and many more by the bottle. There's a good range of smoked fish, salami and salads, an ample, award-winning selection of cheeses and, in winter, at least one or two hot dishes (expect to pay €10-€15). The furniture is basic, the atmosphere calm and collected and the gentle jazz music unobtrusive. Not a place for the rowdies, though the half-price happy hour (a generous 5-8pm) is an excellent way to swot up on Italian vintages. It's good to keep an eye out for the occasional special wine-tasting evenings.

La Vineria

Campo de' Fiori 15 (06 6880 3268). Bus to corso Vittorio Emanuele. **Open** 8.30am-2am Mon-Sat; 5pm-2am Sun. **Credit** AmEx, DC, MC, V.
La Vineria is *the* Roman meeting point: everyone calls in here sooner or later. It's really no more than an authentic local wine bar, but its great location on the campo, young funky staff and low prices make it an evergreen favourite. It was also evocatively portrayed in Michael Dibdin's novel *Vendetta* as the favourite drinking haunt of his cop hero Aurelio Zen. By day and in the early evening it throngs with lived-in locals and expatriates; by night, it's a seriously hip hangout for bright young things (and some slightly tarnished older ones) who join the crush and crowd around its pavement tables.

Mad Jack's

Via Arenula 20 (06 6880 8223). Bus or tram to largo Argentina. **Open** 11am-2am Mon-Thur, Sun; 11am-3am Fri, Sat. Closed 2wks Aug. **Credit** AmEx, DC, MC, V.
A formulaic but reliable Irish tavern in a very central location that's open non-stop throughout the day, every day. At night and especially on weekends, the crowd of young Italians and English-speakers spills out on to the pavement. The beverage of choice here is beer or cider – both available on draught in a range of versions – but there is also an array of wine and cocktails, plus a small selection of bar nibbles. Warning: this can be a depressing place late in the evening if you're over 25.

Sloppy Sam's

Campo de' Fiori 10 (06 6880 2637). Bus to corso Vittorio Emanuele (piazza della Cancelleria). **Open** 4pm-2am daily. **Credit** MC, V.
In a central location on Rome's most buzzing piazza, this American-owned bar has been packing them in for years now. It's got all the basic drinks, but even extends to flavoured Stolichnaya vodkas imported from the US. Everything about the place is loud: the music, the

A legendary Ghetto bakery, tiny **Boccione** (via Portico d'Ottavia 1) turns out rich fruit and nut slabs called (confusingly) pizza, and a truly great torta di ricotta e visciole (ricotta and sour cherry pie).

Latteria del Gallo. *See p104.*

boisterous bartenders, the clientele. English is definitely
the language spoken here, what with all the study-abroad
students and expat faithfuls, so join in the banter over
some drinks, a plate of nachos and maybe a gigantic,
over-stuffed sandwich, and reflect on the fact that this
corner of a foreign land is forever Pittsburgh.

Taverna del Campo

*Campo de' Fiori 16 (06 687 4402). Bus to corso Vittorio
Emanuele (piazza della Cancelleria).* **Open** 9am-2am Tue-
Sun. **Average** €. **Credit** AmEx, DC, MC, V.
A favourite with both Romans and tourists as it's smack
in the middle of campo de' Fiori, this taverna is open all
day and well into the night, has tables outside and serves
everything from a large selection of wines to great pizze
(Roman flatbread sandwiches). Seems like everybody in
town stops by for an aperitivo and a few crostini (mini
savoury toasts with various toppings), and for good

reason. It's handy, it's abustle with life and spirit, and it's a great place to grab a sandwich or salad, or for post-dinner drinks as the piazza overflows with revellers.

The Drunken Ship

Campo de' Fiori 20/21 (06 6830 0535). Bus to corso Vittorio Emanuele (piazza della Cancelleria). **Open** 5pm-2am daily. **Credit** AmEx, MC, V.

This small, modern bar at the northern end of the campo resists the wine bar hegemony. The Drunken Ship stands on a lower but equally important rung of the evolutionary ladder: its main function is to get people drunk, with the help of beer served in pitchers. Large groups of young Americans exchange students hang out here, and there are plenty of happy hour specials to court them. Loud music and DJs keep the ship rolling on its drunken course until late in the night. Hic!

Wine Time

Piazza Pasquale Paoli 15 (06 687 5706). Bus to corso Vittorio Emanuele (Ponte Vittorio Emanuele). **Open** 12.30pm-1.30am Mon-Fri, Sun; 7pm-1.30am Sat. Closed 3wks Aug. **Average** €€. **Credit** AmEx, DC, MC, V.

This new wine bar by the main bridge across to St Peter's is part of a new wave of super-enoteche. It functions as a restaurant for lunch, dinner and Sunday brunch, but also organizes wine tastings with vintners as well as courses on wines (in Italian for the time being – but there may be courses in English soon). A relatively hefty wine list, with 360 mostly Italian labels, is balanced by a limited but adventurous menu. An antipasto of sfogliatine con caprino e mela renetta al timo (puff pastry with goat cheese, apples, thyme and honey) is a sinfully rich beginning to a meal. There are no primi, but there are a number of interesting salads like the insalata Stella, with radicchio, belgian endive, escarole, taleggio cheese and smoked prosciutto served warm, wrapped in a paper bag. For secondi you can go light (turbot fillet with a crust of julienned vegetables), or more substantial (sliced entrecôte steak with rosemary sauce). Finally, the bocciolo di cioccolato fondente (molten chocolate cake), the speciality dolce, will satisfy any chocolate craving.

Bars & cafés

Bella Napoli

Corso Vittorio Emanuele 246 (06 687 7048). Bus to corso Vittorio Emanuele (Chiesa Nuova). **Open** 7.30am-9pm Mon-Fri, Sun. Closed 3wks Aug. **Credit** MC, V.

Best known for its Neapolitan dolci such as sfogliatelle ricce (pastry with ricotta filling), and rum baba, to take away or eat on the spot with a caffè. Have your sfogliatella heated for a real treat. One of the few cafés to have resisted renovation, its rather dingy walls and light fixtures take you back to about 1965.

Bernasconi ★

Piazza Cairoli 16 (06 6880 6264). Bus or tram to via Arenula. **Open** 7am-8.30pm Tue-Sun. Closed Aug. **No credit cards**.

Like so many of Rome's best cake shops, Bernasconi is cramped and inconspicuous, but it's well worth fighting your way inside for the superlative cornetti and excellent cappuccino. Opposite the baroque splendours of San Carlo ai Catinari, yet close to the synagogue, Bernasconi straddles Rome's Jewish and Catholic worlds, with kosher sweets, Lenten cookies and bignè di San Giuseppe (deep-fried, custard-filled buns). The granatine (sugar-sprinkled cakes pumped full of a rich zabaione cream) make for a particularly outstanding dessert.

Caffè Farnese

Via dei Baullari 106 (06 6880 2125). Bus to corso Vittorio Emanuele (piazza della Cancelleria). **Open** 7am-2am daily. **Credit** AmEx, MC, V.

This bar-gelateria/pasticceria is a popular meeting place, offering a fine people-watching vista. It's close to noisy campo de' Fiori but its outside tables have a view of quieter, more harmonious piazza Farnese. The coffee, cornetti and pizza romana here are all excellent.

Da Vezio

Via dei Delfini 23 (06 678 6036). Bus or tram to largo Argentina. **Open** 7.30am-8.15pm Mon-Sat. Closed 3wks Aug. **No credit cards**.

Vezio Bagazzini is a legendary figure in the Ghetto area. Every square centimetre of his extraordinary bar/latteria behind the former Communist Party HQ is filled with Red icons and trophies – Italian, Soviet and Cuban. It used to be that every Italian leftist leader worth his or her salt had his photo taken with Vezio (see the selection on the walls), but in these Blairite times the tradition is waning.

Latteria del Gallo

Vicolo del Gallo 4 (06 686 5091). Bus to corso Vittorio Emanuele. **Open** 8.30am-2.30pm, 5pm-12.30am Mon, Tue, Thur-Sun. Closed 2wks Aug. **No credit cards**.

With its marble slab tables, this café in a side road between campo de' Fiori and piazza Farnese has remained impervious to passing fashions. Behind the bar, Signora Anna serves up her cappuccione – a double, frothy cappuccino – as she has done for decades. A Centro Storico institution, it's still popular with Rome's ageing hippies and foreign residents.

Fiori & Ghetto

Trevi & Veneto

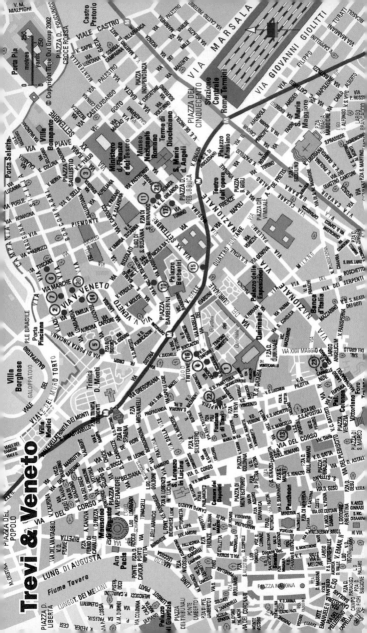

The area around the Quirinal hill and present-day via Veneto was, until well into the 19th century, a place of large princely estates and noble townhouses. The presidential palace on the Quirinale today splits the area into two halves: a low area of medieval streets around the Trevi Fountain (where Anita Ekberg took a dip in Fellini's *La Dolce Vita*), and the rising ground to the north-east centring on another dolce vita icon, via Veneto. Today many of the pricey restaurants and bars in the area can seem rather dated and tired, but in the best, such as **Papà Baccus** (*see p111*) or **Sans Souci** (*also p111*), standards are high and quality is assured.

Restaurants

Al Presidente ★
Via in Arcione 94-5 (06 679 7342). Bus to via del Tritone. **Meals served** 7.30-11.30pm Mon, Wed-Fri; 1-3.30pm, 7.30-11.30pm Sat, Sun. Closed 2wks Aug, 3wks Jan. **Average** €€€. **Credit** DC, MC, V.
This born-again family restaurant under the walls of the Quirinale palace is one of the few really reliable addresses in the Trevi Fountain area. In elegant but restrained surroundings, with well-spaced tables, the Petruccioli clan offers a balance between creativity and tradition in a menu that is strong on seafood. Primi include a creamy zuppa d'asparagi e calamari (asparagus and squid soup), served with a thread of oil; or a good spaghetti con alici e pecorino (with anchovies and pecorino cheese). A secondo of rombo gratinato con carciofi croccanti (rombo au gratin with crunchy artichokes) was also excellent. Desserts such as semifreddo di ricotta con cioccolato e salsa di arancia (ricotta mousse with chocolate orange sauce) are equally convincing. Presentation is a real strong point.

Asador Café Veneto
Via Veneto 116 (06 482 7107). Bus to via Veneto. **Meals served** noon-3pm, 7-11.30pm Tue-Sat. Closed 3wks Aug. **Average** €€€. **Credit** AmEx, DC, MC, V.
One of those glitzy via Veneto restaurants that feature a glassed-in terrace island between pavement and road, Café Veneto is for serious people-watchers and/or serious

Al Presidente. *See p107.*

carnivores. The Italo-Argentine menu showcases the beef of the pampas, but duck, lamb and sausages are also strong points. As a starter, the carpaccio di petto d'anatra (duck breast carpaccio in a sweet mustard sauce) is delicious. Dessert – including the paneneque de manzana alla moda delle pampas (apple crêpes) – are well worth saving space for. A three-course lunch menu that includes wine and coffee is a good deal at €31.

Cantina Cantarini ★

Piazza Sallustio 12 (06 485 528/474 3341). Bus to via XX Settembre. **Meals served** 12.30-3pm, 7.30-11pm Mon-Sat. Closed 2wks Aug, 1wk Christmas. **Average** €€. **Credit** AmEx, DC, MC, V.

This is a high-quality trattoria in a smart neighbourhood, with extraordinarily reasonable prices. The food is Roman but with influences from the Marches, around Urbino. Meat-based for the first part of the week, it turns

fishy from Thursday to Saturday. The atmosphere is as allegro as seating is tight – though outside tables take off some of the pressure in summer. But the excellent coniglio al cacciatore (stewed rabbit), fritto misto di pesce (fried mixed fish) and spaghetti al nero di seppia (with squid ink) should quell concerns about comfort.

Grill & Wine

Via in Arcione 74-5 (06 6992 5457). Bus to via del Tritone. **Meals served** noon-4pm, 5-11.30pm daily. **Average** €€. **Credit** AmEx, DC, MC, V.

The American lava-stone grill (a huge steel affair dominating the entrance) comes to Rome. It's not a bad idea, but this bland modern California-style restaurant is still struggling to find a sense of identity (the piped Elton John soundtrack doesn't help). Still, grilled buffalo fillet makes a change from the usual ossobuco, and the gunmetal-and-wood decor is pleasant enough.

MUSIC LIVES HERE

Hard Rock CAFE

Hard Rock CAFE

ROME

Via Vittorio, 62a/b
Phone: 064203051

La Terrazza dell'Hotel Eden

Via Ludovisi 49 (06 478 121). Bus to via Veneto.
Meals served 12.30-2.30pm, 7.30-10.30pm daily.
Average €€€€€. **Credit** AmEx, DC, MC, V.

One of Rome's most chic and expensive hotels – the Eden – houses one of the city's most chic and expensive restaurants. True to its name, this rooftop eyrie offers a spectacular view of Rome's seven hills. In warm weather, sit out on the pretty terrace; during winter months enjoy the discreet, elegant, minimalist decor, which competes as little as possible with that widescreen vista. Enrico Derflingher, once Princess Diana's personal chef, has a mod-Med approach based on fresh, flavourful dishes that shirk heavy sauces; the fegato d'anatra (duck's liver), in particular, is divine. If the price of a meal is out of your range, the attached bar is also an ideal place for a pre-dinner aperitivo. If you opt to throw frugality to the winds and eat, dinner reservations are essential.

Papà Baccus ★

Via Toscana 36 (06 4274 2808). Bus to via Boncompagni.
Meals served 12.30-3pm, 7.30-11.30pm Mon-Fri; 7.30pm-midnight Sat. Closed 1wk Aug. **Average** €€€. **Credit** AmEx, DC, MC, V.

This is Tuscan cuisine at its best. All the raw materials, from the olive oil to the excellent hams and salamis, are imported from owner Italo Cipriani's native Casentino valley. For starters, try the ribollita, a delicious soup made from beans, fresh vegetables and bread, or the sfoglia di caciotta toscana primosale (layers of cheese and anchovy with a spinach, pear and walnut salad). The rombo (turbot) – served with artichokes – and the baccalà (salt cod) are also good bets, though the real forté here is the Chianina beef. Served with zolfino beans or simply seared, this is what eating fillet should be about.

Sans Souci

Via Sicilia 20 (06 4201 4510). Bus to Via Veneto.
Meals served 8-11pm daily. Closed 2wks Aug.
Average €€€€€. **Credit** AmEx, DC, MC, V.

This restaurant has long been a favourite with Roman glitterati and well-heeled foreigners. Carved wood-beam ceilings, chandeliers and old mirrors set the grand tone. A standard menu is supplemented by more creative specials. A rich antipasto of petto di piccione sauté con escalope di fois gras al tartufo di Norcia (sautéd pigeon breast and fois gras in a black truffle sauce) has a deep, woody flavour, while grilled costolette di agnello con salvia e limone (lamb chops with sage and lemon) are sweet, well seasoned and perfectly cooked. Skip the tired dessert cart and treat yourself to an aged distillato instead – or another bottle from the excellent wine list.

La Terrazza dell'Hotel Eden. *See p111.*

A multi-function bakery, grocery and snack bar right next to the Trevi Fountain, **L'Antico Forno** (via delle Muratte 8) does a good line in fresh filled rolls and takeaway pizza.

The best food in town

La Pergola
See p197.

Il Convivio
See p57.

Agata e Romeo
See p170.

Il Leonardo
See p199.

Papà Baccus
See p111.

Tullio

Via San Nicola da Tolentino 26 (06 474 5560).
Meals served 12.30-3pm, 7.30-11pm Mon-Sat.
Closed Aug. **Average** €€€. **Credit** AmEx, DC, MC, V.
Just off piazza Barberini, this crowded restaurant has been
serving Tuscan fare to a mixed clientele of business types
and media celebrities for decades. The heavy oak interior
gives the place the feel of a gentlemen's club. The menu
offers Tuscan fundamentals: ribollita (a hearty bread
soup), fagioli all'olio (white beans in olive oil) and the
classic bistecca alla fiorentina (Florentine steak), plus a few
Roman dishes like vignarola (broad bean, pea and ham
soup). There is also a good selection of fresh fish. The
service is ultra-professional; the ample wine list is strong
on Tuscan and Piedmontese reds. The only downside is
the decidedly high prices.

Vivendo

St Regis Grand Hotel, via VE Orlando 3 (06 4709 2736).
Metro Repubblica/bus to piazza della Repubblica. **Meals**
served 7.30-10.30pm Tue-Sun. **Average** €€€€€.
Credit AmEx, DC, MC, V.
The rediscovery of the Roman hotel restaurant, part three.
Inspired by the success of Enrico Derflingher at the Hotel
Eden (La Terrazza, *see p111*) and the triumph of Heinz
Beck at the Hilton (La Pergola, *see p197*), the Starwood
group hired chef Umberto Vezzoli to bring a Michelin star
home to roost at Vivendo, the restaurant of the newly
refurbished St Regis Grand. The long, low restaurant
offers a modern take on the Ancient Roman banqueting
hall – gilded Corinthian columns, lilac and cream drapes,
burnished silver chairs. In these relaxing surroundings,

Papà Baccus. *See p11:*

an efficient team serves up Vezzoli's ambitious (at times overambitious) creations, which might include linguine all'astice e mela verde (with lobster and green apple) or giambonetto di coniglio aromatizzato al lardo e rosmarino (rabbit drumstick with bacon fat and rosemary). The wine list is extensive and refreshingly international, and wines by the glass are also available – a rarity in this price range.

Wine bars & pubs

Antica Birreria ★
Via di San Marcello 19 (06 679 5310). Bus to piazza Venezia. **Meals served** noon-midnight daily. Closed 2wks Aug. **Average** €. **Credit** AmEx, MC, V.
Much better known by its traditional name, Birreria Peroni, this is the perfect place for a quick but wholesome lunch or pre/post-cinema dinner. Service is canteen-style, and the food – three or four hot pasta options, salmon, sausages, caprese salads – is good and cheap. The birreria still retains its original art nouveau decor, with a chiaroscuro frieze featuring slogans like 'drink beer and you'll live 100 years'. At lunchtime, avoid the 1pm rush, when you have to push in past the row of regulars eating their pasta standing up at the bar. There are four beers on draught.

Vineria Il Chianti

Via del Lavatore 81-2 (06 678 7550). Bus to via del Tritone. **Open** 10am-2.30am Mon-Sat. **Meals served** 12.30-3.30pm, 7.15-11pm Mon-Sat. Closed Aug. **Average** €-€€. **Credit** AmEx, DC, MC, V.

As the name suggests, wine, food and decor all have a Tuscan slant here – though the service is young, brisk and Roman. The typical lunch menu might feature a couple of

Get serious about pasta

One of Rome's few private museums, the Museo Nazionale delle Paste Alimentari is dedicated to the most prevalent food in Italy. It could easily be accused of offering too much information, but, for serious pasta buffs, this palazzo near the Trevi Fountain is probably a must-see.

It does offer some interesting information. The myth that it was Marco Polo who brought spaghetti back from China, for instance, is dashed by a copy of a document dating from 1154, in which Arab geographer Al Idrisi writes admiringly of the Sicilian durum wheat fields, whose proto-pasta products were exported around the western Mediterranean.

There is plenty of pasta machinery on show here, from a primitive Ligurian gramola (kneader) with a huge marble wheel to advanced factory extruders. Diagrams plot the changes pasta undergoes during cooking, and illustrate the nutritional benefits of eating one's pasta al dente – still with a little bite to it – rather than boiled to mush in the Anglo-Saxon style.

The museum has a number of examples of the genre paintings and sketches known as 'Maccheroni eaters' – showing peasant folk wolfing down ropeloads of spaghetti – which became popular Grand Tour souvenirs. Paparazzi shots of pasta-gobbling film stars like Totò and Sophia Loren continued the tradition.

There is some rather dubious modern art on a pasta theme, two miniature 'pasta theatres' designed by artist Antonio Rubino, and even a poster suggesting that pasta could be the answer to the Third World's food problems, with the cheery legend 'pasta: where hope lies'.

The museum also acts as a centre of pasta research, organising seminars and promoting an annual prize for those who have distinguished themselves in the field of, you guessed it, pasta.

Museo Nazionale delle Paste Alimentari

Piazza Scanderbeg 117 (06 699 1199). **Open** 9.30am-5.30pm daily. **Admission** €7.75; €4.65 concessions. **No credit cards.**

Antica Birreria. *See p114.*

filling grain and bean soups, a pasta dish such as ravioli con i fiori di zucca (ravioli topped with courgette flowers) and a meaty secondo such as abbacchio scottadito (grilled lamb chops). Pizzas make an appearance in the evening. The retro rustic room is dominated by wine: in glass-fronted cabinets and wooden wine cases.

Bars & cafés

Café de Paris
Via Veneto 90 (06 488 5284). Metro Barberini/bus to via Veneto. **Open** 8.30am-2am daily. **Credit** AmEx, DC, MC, V.

gourmet value

Uno e Bino
See p201.

Antico Arco
See p135.

Al Presidente
See p107.

Il Gonfalone
See p91.

Boccondivino
See p55.

In via Veneto's 1960s heyday, Café Doney (*see p120*) across the road was for the nobs, while this place was for those with street-cred. Here you could be served in your jeans (quite something in those days), and watch the paparazzi hunt down their celebrity prey. There's little anything-cred about it now: American-style breakfast is served in the morning to American tourists, English tea is served in the afternoon to English tourists, and the international-style wine bar brings in tourists from everywhere in the evening.

Caffetteria Borromini

Via XX Settembre 124 (06 488 0866). Bus to piazza Barberini/via Nazionale. **Open** 7.30am-8pm Mon-Fri, 7.30am-2pm Sat. *Meals served* 12.30-3pm Mon-Fri, 12.30am-2pm Sat. Closed 1wk Aug. **Credit** AmEx, MC, V.
This multipurpose bar, trattoria, tabaccheria and official lottery outlet has grown over the years from a tiny underground bar with one dining room out back to become a huge lunchtime food factory occupying three vast, vaulted rooms. This is cheap Italian fast food at its best, with two pasta choices, plenty of secondi and real wood-fired pizza, a rarity at lunchtime. All is served with breathtaking efficiency to hordes of hungry office workers.

Caffè Traforo

Via del Traforo 135 (06 482 2946). Bus to via del Tritone. **Open** 6am-9pm Mon-Sat. **Credit** MC, V.
The owners have renovated this spot dear to the hearts of clerks from local banks and reporters from *Il Messaggero's* offices around the corner, but the cherrywood panelling and green Brazilian marble have remained the same. The caffè Traforo and cappuccino Traforo – creamy caffeine

Dagnino

concoctions with secret ingredients – are legendary. It's a crowded, lively spot at noon, when there's a cold buffet and a good assortment of sandwiches, fruit shakes and sweets.

Dagnino ★

Galleria Esedra, via VE Orlando 75 (06 481 8660). Metro Repubblica. **Open** 7am-10pm daily. **Credit** AmEx, MC, V. Stunning 1950s decor and a chronic oversupply of tables set the scene for this corner of Sicily in Rome. If you can eat it or drink it and it's Sicilian, it's here: ice-cream in special buns, almond drinks, marzipan fruits. Regulars come for the crisp cannoli siciliani filled with ricotta and, above all, for the baroque splendour of the shiny green-iced cassata, uniting all the flavours of the south: the perfume of candied citrus and almond paste, and the fresh saltiness of ricotta.

Doney

Via Veneto 145 (06 4708 2805). Metro Barberini.
Open 8am-midnight Tue-Sun. **Credit** AmEx DC, MC, V.
This historic via Veneto watering hole is a throwback to
the days when fare l'americano was the height of every
young Italian blade's aspirations. It's still popular with
both locals and tourists, whether for stand-up coffee or
to watch via Veneto traffic go past over a dry martini.
Doney had its place in the sun in the 1950s and '60s, when
it was a key meeting point for the Cinecittà set (Ava
Gardner, Marcello Mastroianni, Tyrone Power, Anita
Ekberg) and the Roman intelligentsia.

Le Grand Bar

*St Regis Grand Hotel, via VE Orlando 3 (06 4709). Metro
Repubblica/bus to piazza Repubblica.* **Open** 10am-1am
daily. **Credit** AmEx, DC, MC, V.
This gorgeous lobby bar is everything one might expect
at a hotel of this echelon. Its plush red velvet banquettes,
marble walls and romantic palm plants lend it the feel of
an exotic 1940s movie set. Tuxedo-clad barman Massimo
Azzurro is a true old-style cocktail professional. The bar
tab will help to bring you back to earth: it's €14 for a
martini and €6 for a glass of plain old mineral water.
Afternoon teas and light lunches are also on offer.

News Café

*Via della Stamperia 72 (06 6992 3473). Metro
Barberini.* **Open** *Oct-Mar* 7am-9pm Mon-Thur;
7am-1am Fri; 9am-1am Sat; 11am-8pm Sun. *Apr-Sept*
7am-1am daily. **Credit** AmEx, MC, V.
This New York-style bar with modern steel-and-wood
decor plays lip service to the 'news' theme with racks of
papers and a 24-hour satellite news screen. But behind
the façade it's a regular Roman bar with better than
average lunch options (salads, soups, pasta, filled rolls)
and cakes – including those, erm, Roman classics,
muffins and brownies. The service can be a little offhand
if you're not a regular, and the seating is cramped – unless
you manage to secure one of the few outside tables.

Rockodile

*Via delle Tre Cannelle 9 (06 678 7771). Bus to
Piazza Venezia/Via Nazionale.* **Open** 8pm-2.30am daily.
Credit AmEx, DC, MC, V.
This 'southern California-style' bar/pub is an outpost for
both expats and Italians. There are several rooms, all in
dark wood with dim lighting: the front bar, a side room
with cozy banquettes, and a back room with bar tables,
stools and a dancefloor where a DJ spins tunes at
weekends. It even has a 'VIP' area upstairs, where tables
can be reserved. In warm weather there are tables out
front and on the side steps leading up to the Quirinale.

Vatican, Prati & West

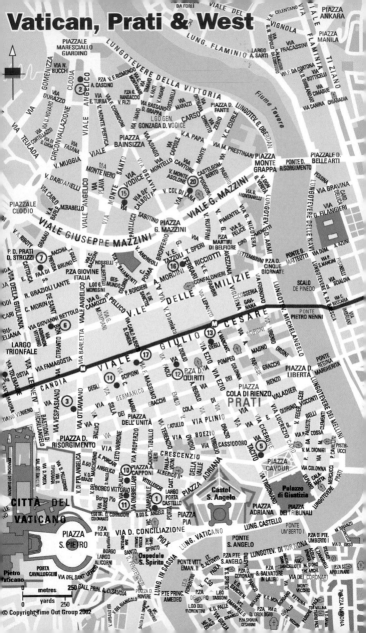

The Vatican's influence on the cuisine of Rome is limited these days to a preference for fish on Fridays, seasonal cakes (like the Easter colomba) and the occasional appearance on menus of the hand-rolled spaghetti known as strozzapreti (priest-stranglers). The Holy See is surrounded to the north and north-east by an area of Risorgimento grid-plan streets known as Prati, a lively, upmarket shopping and residential quartiere with good eating and drinking options. Elegant cafés and pasticcerie are a particular forte – especially around the media hub of piazza Mazzini. Due west of St Peter's, Borgo was decimated by Mussolini in the 1930s to provide a suitably triumphant approach to the basilica. Hungry pilgrims and Swiss Guards are not the best spur to culinary excellence, but a couple of new openings in the area provide a ray of hope.

Vatican, Prati & West

Restaurants

Borgo Antico ★
Borgo Pio 21 (06 686 5967). Bus to via Vitelleschi or via della Conciliazione. **Meals served** 8pm-midnight Mon-Wed; 8pm-1am Thur-Sat. Closed 3wks Aug. **Average** €€. **Credit** AmEx, V, MC.
Goethe said that 'life is too short to drink mediocre wines', and his words are taken seriously at Borgo Antico. Describing itself as a 'typical 17th-century tavern,' this rustic, wood-beamed hostelry offers an extensive selection of wines to be savoured together with a selection of gastronomic delights from different Italian regions. Many of the wines are also available by the glass. No pasta or pizza here: instead there are cold platters covered with salamis from Umbria and Valle d'Aosta, a selection of cheeses matured in a variety of interesting ways, and smoked fish. Hot dishes might include the likes of polenta served with porcini mushrooms, truffles, wild boar or hare sauce or grilled scamorza cheese with radicchio.

Dal Toscano al Girarrosto

Candido

Viale Angelico 275-77 (06 3751 7704). Bus to viale Angelico. **Meals served** 12.30-3pm, 7.30pm-midnight Mon, Wed-Sun. Closed 2wks Aug. **Average** €€. **Credit** AmEx, DC, MC, V.

Pizza, pasta, fish, meat – you name it, they've got it in this bustling, typically Roman restaurant. The menu has been translated into English so you can be sure whether you've ordered your noodles with egg and bacon (alla carbonara) or with artichokes (con carciofi); but it's also worth asking if there are any daily specials – such as the polenta with sausage and tomato sauce. The selection of fried antipasti (fritto misto italiana) leaves a lot to be desired; better leap straight to pasta, or order a crisp Roman-style pizza and a glass of the on-tap red wine – a mellow Montepulciano. Booking is strongly advised.

Dal Toscano al Girarrosto

Via Germanico 58-60 (06 3972 5717/www.ristorante daltoscano.it). Metro Ottaviano/bus or tram to piazza del Risorgimento. **Meals served** 12.30-3pm, 8-11.30pm Tue-Sun. Closed 1wk Dec, 2wks Aug. **Average** €€. **Credit** AmEx, DC, MC, V.

The raw slabs of beef on display here make Dal Toscano's mission clear from the outset: don't expect to find any fish, just plenty of meat – boiled, grilled or fried. The restaurant first opened its doors in 1938 just down

Two addresses for quick snacks near the Vatican: get rolls and simple pasta dishes at Paninoteca da Guido (Borgo Pio 13), and better-than-average takeaway pizza from Mediterraneo (via delle Grazie 7-9).

the street from the Vatican, and the decor and menu
haven't changed since. Dressed in white tuxedo jackets,
the all-male waiting staff serve up solid portions of
bistecca all fiorentina (Florentine steak) with quasi-
religious solemnity. The wide selection of classic Tuscan
primi including ribollita (bread and vegetable soup) or
fettuccine ai funghi porcini (with porcini mushrooms)
provide a decent meatless alternative. It's a popular
place, especially with TV folk and the local bourgeoisie.
So book ahead if you want to be sure of joining them.

Il Bar sotto il Mare

*Via Santamaura 88 (06 3973 8954). Metro Ottaviano/
bus to via Andrea Doria.* **Meals served** 8.30-11.30pm
Tue-Sat. Closed 2wks Aug. **Average** €€-€€€. **Credit**
AmEx, MC, V.

This family run seafood restaurant in a street almost
opposite the entrance to the Vatican museums would
be perfectly placed for post-Sistine Chapel refuelling
were it not for the evening-only opening hours. It offers
unusual pasta combinations such as tagliatelle con
zucca e mazzancolle (with pumpkin and prawns) and
tagliolini con pesto e vongole (with pesto and clams),
as well as a starter plate of oysters and raw shellfish,
served on ice. Leave some room for the fruit sorbets,
served inside a scooped-out fruit – an Amalfi Coast
speciality. With giant seashell lightshades the decor
borders on kitsch, and there are too many tables in too
small a space; but prices are reasonable and the service
extremely friendly.

Il Simposio ★

Piazza Cavour 16 (06 321 1502). Bus to piazza Cavour.
Meals served 1-2.30pm, 8-11.15pm Mon-Fri; 8-11.15pm
Sat. Closed Aug. **Average** €€€. **Credit** AmEx, DC,
MC, V.

With its plush seating, refined decor and upscale cuisine
(and prices), this place is more a full-scale restaurant
than a wine bar. For a starter try the simple but tasty
double artichoke antipasto: served either alla romana
(that is, braised and stuffed with a minty mixture of
herbs), or alla giudia (deep fried). The primi juxtapose
traditional dishes such as spaghetti all'amatriciana with
more innovative creations, like the potato and white
bean soup with goat cheese croutons. Main courses are
mostly meat- and game-based; for example, a guinea
fowl breast wrapped in lardo di Colonnata, served with
a blood orange sauce. Perhaps most unusual at Il
Simposio is the foie gras menu – try the strudel di pere
e foie gras (pear and fois gras pie) – a delicious
combination of red wine-poached pear and rich, pastry-
encased fois gras.

Osteria dell'Angelo ★

Via Giovanni Bettolo 24 (06 372 9470). Metro
Ottaviano/bus to via Ottaviano. **Meals served**
8-11pm Mon, Wed, Thur-Sat; 1-2.30pm, 8-11pm Tue, Fri.
Closed Aug. **Average €€. No credit cards**.

Angelo Croce's neighbourhood trattoria – situated five
minute's walk north of the Vatican – is a real one-off,
just like the man himself. It's decorated with photos of
boxers and rugby players – the twin sporting passions
of Angelo and his culinary helpmates. The menu –
which, in the evening, comes at a fixed price of €21 a
head, rough and ready house wine included – celebrates
the Roman tradition in dishes such as the tonnarelli
cacio e pepe (among the best in town) and another of
meatballs flavoured with nutmeg, pine nuts and
sultanas. Dessert at Osteria dell'Angelo consists of a
glass of romanella (sweet wine) and ciambelline
(aniseed biscuits).

Siciliainbocca

Via Faà di Bruno 26 (06 3735 8400). Metro
Ottaviano/bus to viale Angelico. **Meals served** 1-3pm,
8pm-midnight Mon-Sat. Closed 2wks Aug. **Average €€€.**
Credit AmEx, DC, MC, V.

This new Sicilian restaurant north of the Vatican proved a
huge hit with locals almost from day one. It's easy to see
why: the ambience is allegro, there are tables outside and
there is a sunny lemon theme throughout – even on the
waiters' uniforms. The mixed sfizi dell'isola starter
(aubergines, sun-dried tomatoes, olives) is good, and first
courses are competent, with one of the best being the
conchiglie Vecchia Taormina (pasta shells with peas, broad
beans and pecorino cheese). Some secondi, like the calamari
ripieni (stuffed squid), are uninspired, unfortunately, but,
among the desserts, the cassata – a classic Sicilian ricotta
and candied fruit concoction – stands out.

Taverna Angelica

Piazza Amerigo Capponi 6 (06 687 4514). Bus to piazza
Risorgimento/via Vitelleschi. **Meals served** 7.30pm-
12.30am daily. **Average €€€. Credit** AmEx, MC, V.

This is one of the few stylishly creative eateries within easy
range of the Vatican. The acoustics here are not conducive
to a quiet evening out, but the food is imaginative and well
presented, the wine list extensive and the service friendly.
Tasty starters include a triptych of marinated or smoked
fish (swordfish, octopus and salmon) or duck (tartare,
smoked breast and roast), while the pasta course includes
risottos with smoked eel (anguilla affumicata) or with
sausage and wild endive (scarola e luganica). There is also
a wide selection of cheeses and some unusual desserts,
including fresh dates filled with coffee cream.

Siciliainbocca

Velando ★

Borgo Vittorio 26 (06 6880 9955). Bus to piazza Risorgimento or via di Porta Castello. **Meals served** noon-3pm, 7.30-11pm Mon-Sat. **Average** €€€. **Credit** AmEx, DC, MC, V.

The traditional dishes and nouvelle cuisine from the Val Camonica region of northern Italy, carefully prepared and elegantly served here, are understandably popular with bishops and cardinals from the large religious organisation up the street. Be prepared to expand your mind and your taste buds with delicacies like risotto alle fragoline di bosco (wild strawberry risotto) and strudel con rana e verdure (yes, that's frog and vegetable strudel), or stick to more traditional recipes based on freshwater fish such as coregone or the local caprino goat's cheese. Leave room for one of the rich and creamy bavarese desserts.

Pizzerie

La Pratolina ★

Via degli Scipioni 248-250 (06 3600 4409). Metro Ottaviano/bus to viale Giulio Cesare. **Meals served** 7.30pm-midnight daily. Closed 2wks Aug. **Average** €. **Credit** AmEx, DC, MC, V.

Halfway along an interminable residential Prati street stands this cheap and cheerful pizzeria with a difference. The pizzas are made from a dough that is left to rise for 48 hours before being flattened into an oval-shaped 'pinza degli dei', resembling an ancient Roman type of unleavened bread. Toppings vary from the tasty gorgonzola and radicchio to the unlikely sausage, potato and truffle. Starters include a selection of crispy fried vegetables and cheeses, while those with a sweet tooth should not miss the heavenly coconut mousse served with lashings of nutella and pine nuts.

International

Zen ★

Via degli Scipioni 243 (06 321 3420/www.zenworld.it).
Metro Lepanto/bus to viale Giulio Cesare. **Meals served**
1-3pm, 8.30-11pm Tue-Fri, Sun; 8.30-11pm Sat. Closed
2wks Aug. **Average** €€. **Credit** AmEx, DC, MC, V.
Just around the corner from the Lepanto metro stop, this recently opened offshoot of a successful Milanese sushi bar was a thriving concern right from the start. The atmosphere is modern, with obtrusive steel ventilator ducts. In the centre of the room is Rome's first sushi and sashimi conveyor belt. There are tables around the sides of the belt, or, for less hustle and bustle, you can sit in a large back room. More substantial meals include the sashimi boat, noodles or seared tuna. Zen has set a new standard for high-quality, affordable Japanese food in Rome – so come early or book ahead.

Wine bars

Del Frate ★

Via degli Scipioni 118 (06 323 6437). Metro Ottaviano.
Meals served 12.30pm-1am Mon-Sat. Closed 10 days
Aug. **Average** €€. **Credit** AmEx, DC, MC, V.
This historic Prati wine shop expanded into a wine bar annexe a couple of years ago and has since built up a loyal following. Its atmosphere is truly Italian, as wooden tables spill over into the enoteca, amid high cherrywood shelves crammed with bottles of wine. Not only can you sip from a lovely bottle of wine, but the food is impressive as well. A dish like the ravishing ravioli cotti al forno di salmone in crema di zucchine (oven-baked ravioli with salmon and courgette sauce) is a good demonstration of the chef's modern Italian flair. The only off-note is the steep mark-up on wines: almost triple what the same bottle would cost to take away (especially painful if you happen to be staring at it on the shelf).

For everything from Vialone Nano risotto rice to Vegemite to Vietnamese fish sauce: Castroni (via Cola di Rienzo 196) is Rome's best-stocked international deli.

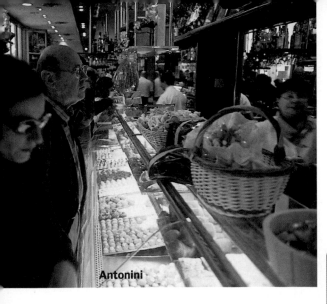
Antonini

Bars & cafés

Antonini
Via Sabotino 21-9 (06 3751 7845). Bus to piazza Mazzini.
Open 7am-9pm daily. **Credit** MC, V.
In winter you can't move for fur coats in here, as this high-class pasticceria is the place in Rome to buy cakes. There are air kisses and sugar everywhere you turn in here, but, if you can bear it, the rewards are sweet as well. For example, the montebianco, with meringue, marron glacé, spaghetti and cream is absolutely spectacular. There's also a nice line in tartine here, as the canapés topped with pâté or caviar are in very high demand. Loll at one of the pavement tables for insight into the lives of the Roman bourgeoisie and their mobile phones.

Faggiani ★
Via G Ferrari 23-9 (06 3973 9742). Bus to piazza Mazzini. **Open** 6.30am-9pm Mon, Tue; 6.30am-8pm Thur-Sun. Closed 2wks Aug. **Credit** AmEx, MC, V.
As pleasant for breakfast as for an evening aperitivo, this classic family bar with excellent coffee has the added attraction of being attached to one of Rome's finest pasticcerie. It's worth coming all the way to Prati, even if you're miles away, just to sample the cornetti and budino di riso (sweet rice-filled tartlets), which are probably the best in Rome.

Tramonti e Muffati
See p208.

Del Frate
See p128.

Cul de Sac
See p72.

Cavour 313
See p186.

Il Goccetto
See p99.

NapulArte

Via Fabio Massimo 113 (06 323 1005). Metro Ottaviano/bus to via Fabio Massimo. **Open** 7am-2am daily. **Credit** AmEx, DC, MC, V.

Opened at the end of 2001, this Neapolitan bar-pizzeria, down a flight of steps from the road, is run by a lively, if rather gruff, family. They do a good range of traditional Italian pastries, just the way mama used to make them. Best are their Neapolitan cakes such as sfogliatelle (layers of crispy pastry with ricotta inside), babà (sponge cake soaked in rum) and pastiera napoletana (flan filled with ricotta, softened cereal grains and orange-water – definitely an acquired taste). If you want an excuse to stop by here, you can also pop in for a cheap light meal of pasta or thick-crust Neapolitan pizzas.

Vanni

Via Col di Lana 10 (06 322 3642). Bus to piazza Mazzini. **Open** 7am-midnight daily. **Credit** AmEx, DC, MC, V.

This classic Prati bar is much frequented by media folk, as state broadcaster Rai has offices and studios in the area. Of course, trust journalists to know where the good food is. Over the years Vanni has become a north Rome catering empire, but this is its primary venue for catering to yourself. It offers a full range of goodies, from practically perfect morning cornetti through to a divine lunchtime self-service buffet (L'Arcipelago), passing via afternoon tea to aperitivi and cocktails, accompanied by excellent savoury tartine (canapés), and finally on to the evening's pizzas, grilled meat and seafood. The prices are generally affordable, the atmosphere friendly (if busy) and the food is very good.

Vatican, Prati & West

Trastevere
& Monteverde

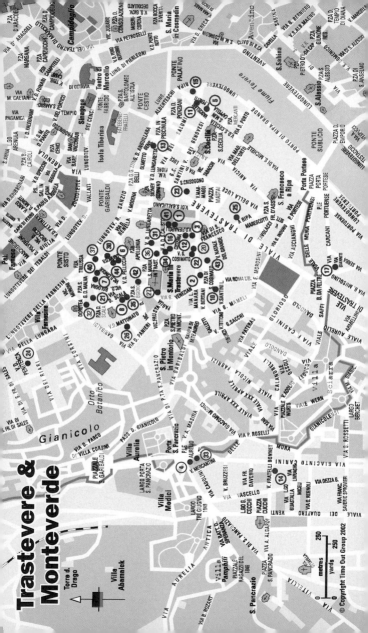

Literally 'across the Tiber', Trastevere is Rome's Left Bank. This proud and picturesque working-class district has come to represent the quintessence of all that is truly Roman, despite the fact that the trasteverini like to stress their differences from their Centro Storico cousins across the river. Although the area has been colonised by expatriates and wine bars, there is still a strong local community here; in the small hours, homeward-bound ravers cross paths with market traders heading out to work. Trastevere has one of the highest concentrations of busy bars and restaurants of any quartiere, but you should be selective, as slapdash, overpriced tourist-traps abound. Recently, there has been an upswing in the area's culinary fortunes, with the opening of good high-level restaurants and more affordable creative trattorie.

Trastevere & Monteverde

Restaurants

Ai Fienaroli
Via dei Fienaroli 5 (06 588 4474). Bus/tram to viale Trastevere. **Meals served** 12.30-3pm, 8-11.30pm Mon-Sat. Closed 2wks Aug, 2wks Jan. **Average** €€. **Credit** AmEx, DC, V.

A young chef opened this clean, NY-style place a year ago. His soft fusion approach is exemplified in an antipasto of *cervice di gamberi e spigola marinati con coriandolo, lime e arancio* (raw marinated prawns and sea bass with coriander, lime and orange juice), and a primo of *gnocchi di patate con gamberi sfumati al cognac e salsa di broccoli* (potato dumplings with prawns steamed in cognac and broccoli sauce). Secondi, on the other hand, might include a Japanese-leaning *tataki di tonno* (seared tuna). The young, helpful staff can explain the more outlandish dishes, although only the brave will want to order some of them. Those with no shame can finish up with the 'chocolate sin', a calorific chocolate bombe; the more demure might like to try the *marquis al cioccolato con gelato di riso e croccante di mandorle* (chocolate marquis with rice ice-cream and almonds).

Alberto Ciarla ★

Piazza San Cosimato 40 (06 581 8668/www.alberto ciarla.com). Tram to viale Trastevere. **Meals served** 8.30pm-midnight Mon-Sat. Closed 1wk Aug, 1wk Jan. **Average** €€€€. **Credit** AmEx, DC, MC, V.

The reputation of this owner-named restaurant is stuck in the same 1960s timewarp as the decor, which makes the place look like a rather dubious club privé. But these guys certainly know how to cook. In fact, Alberto Ciarla challenges La Rosetta for the title of Rome's best fish restaurant – and a meal here is a whole lot more affordable, especially if you opt for one of the taster menus. A trademark dish like spigola con le erbe (sea bass with herbs) strikes the right balance between art and nature, while a primo of pasta e fagioli con le cozze (pasta and beans with mussels) is strong, decisive and very Roman. The menu is a triumph of Dolce Vita typography; the overriding mood one of charmingly courteous camp.

Alle Fratte di Trastevere ★

Via delle Fratte di Trastevere 49/50 (06 583 5775). Tram to viale Trastevere. **Meals served** *Sept-Apr* 12.30-3pm, 6.30-11.30pm Mon, Tue, Thur-Sun. *May-Aug* 6.30pm-1.30am Mon, Tue, Thur-Sun. **Average** €€. **Credit** AmEx, DC, MC, V.

Trastevere has its fair share of traditional, family-run trattorie, but this cheap and cheerful place has got to be one of the best. It does honest, well-executed Roman trattoria fare with Neapolitan influences, and the service is friendly, attentive and bilingual (the owner's wife comes from Long Island). For starters, the carpaccio di polipo con la rucola ai profumi di agrumi (thinly sliced

The best breakfast bar

La Caffetiera
See p78.

Sacchetti
See p154.

Faggiani
See p129.

Bar della Pace
See p77.

Linari
See 166.

Augusto. *See p136.*

octopus on a bed of rocket with citrus-scented dressing) is a winner. First courses like pennette alla Sorrentina (penne pasta with tomatoes and mozzarella) are served up in generous portions. Secondi include oven-roasted sea bream, veal escalopes in marsala sauce, and a good grilled beef fillet. Desserts are made on-site, and the post-prandial digestivi flow freely.

Antico Arco ★

Piazzale Aurelio 7 (06 581 5274). Bus to via Carini.
Meals served 7.30pm-midnight Mon-Sat. Closed 3wks Aug. **Average** €€€. **Credit** AmEx, DC, MC, V.
Dinner at this relaxed creative Italian restaurant on the Gianicolo hill – right behind porta San Pancrazio – is always a pleasure, and still represents excellent value for money. The soothing modern decor makes up for the lack of a view, and the service is attentive, affable and multi-lingual. The menu is strong on all fronts, from the antipasti (an outstanding tortino di cipolle con crema di grana – onion flan with grana cheese sauce) to the primi (where classics like the risotto with Castelmagno cheese are flanked by innovations such as the ravioli ripieni di patate e calamari con dadolata di olive taggiasche – large ravioli filled with potatoes and squid, in an olive broth) to the secondi, which stretch from meat to fish to game (quaglia disossata in sfoglia di patate e rosmarino – deboned quail in a potato and rosemary case). The choreographic desserts are no letdown; and Maurizio, the

sommelier, can help steer a course through the extensive, well-priced wine list. It's hugely popular, so book at least a couple of days in advance.

Asinocotto

Via dei Vascellari 48 (06 589 8985). Tram to piazza Sonnino/bus to Isola Tiberina. **Meals served** *Oct-Apr* 8-11pm Tue-Sat; 12.45-2.30pm, 8-11pm Sun. *May-Sept* 8-11pm Tue-Sun. Closed Jan. **Average** €€€. **Credit** AmEx, DC, MC, V.

Giuliano Brenna, one time protégé of Princess Diana's chef, works small miracles in the tiny kitchen of this gay-friendly foodie mecca at the quiet end of Trastevere. Having a fairly restricted, seasonally changing menu helps, and although Brenna has his off-days and off-dishes, he can also get it spectacularly right, as in the tagliatelle al radicchio e fave (a bitter red lettuce and broad bean sauce) or the garganelli alla triglia e zafferano (fresh penne with a red mullet and saffron sauce). Fish takes a front seat, with novel main courses like cernia al mandarino e molluschi ai carciofi (fillet of grouper with a mandarin and mussel sauce served with artichokes). The wine cellar here is well stocked.

Augusto

Piazza de' Renzi 15 (06 580 3798). Tram to viale Trastevere. **Meals served** noon-3pm, 8-11pm Mon-Sat. Closed mid Aug-mid Sept. **Average** €. **No credit cards**.

This place is like a 'traditional Roman' movie cliché, especially in summer, when its wooden tables covered with simple paper tablecloths spill out into a pretty neighbourhood square in the heart of Trastevere. True to the look, Augusto serves classics of Roman cuisine such as rigatoni all'amatriciana, pasta e lenticchie (pasta with lentils) and pollo arrosto con patate (roast chicken with potatoes) at affordable prices. It rests a little too much on its reputation, and service can be on the rude side of slapdash – but after you've downed that carafe of honest red wine, it will all seem terrifically folkloristico, as the locals say.

Checco er Carrettiere

Via Benedetta 10/13 (06 581 7018/580 0985). Bus to piazza Trilussa. **Meals served** 12.30-2.30pm, 8-11pm Mon-Sat; 1-3pm Sun. **Average** €€-€€€. **Credit** AmEx, DC, MC, V.

This Trastevere restaurant is a throwback to Rome's Hollywood on the Tiber days when film people from Federico Fellini to Henry Fonda piled in for classics like bombolotti alla matriciana (with tangy tomato and bacon) or spaghetti alla carbonara (with egg and bacon). Their pictures line the walls; the other salient feature of the decor is garlic, which hangs in un-ironic strings from a

Sandwich collectors can head for La Casa del Tramezzino (viale Trastevere 81), where over 100 varieties are available.

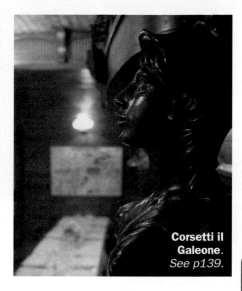

Corsetti il Galeone.
See p139.

high wood-beamed ceiling. These days, Checco is still good for hearty high-octane Roman cuisine. The helpings are huge, the service friendly, and the Frascati house wine is surprisingly smooth and drinkable. In summer, tables spill out into a cool courtyard.

Cibus ★
Via della Scala 8 (06 581 6317). Bus to piazza Trilussa.
Meals served 7.30-11.30pm Mon-Sat. Closed 2wks Aug.
Average €€-€€€. **Credit** AmEx, DC, MC, V.
This creative Italian diner is a refreshing addition to a Trastevere restaurant scene that is dominated by downmarket, touristy pizzerie and trattorie. Cibus (it means 'food' in Latin) has been open for over a year now, and its initially high prices have come down quite a bit, making this a good mid-range option. Pleasant background music, friendly and helpful service, and modern country house decor are bonuses. The food itself is carefully prepared updated Italian fare, taking in an antipasto of crochette di baccala su purea di ceci (salt cod fritters on a chickpea purée) and pasta courses such as a saucy fusilli all'amatriciana, or giant rigatoni with a duck, mushroom and black truffle sauce; secondi – if you make it that far – include a good roast pork 'alla parmigiana'. The elaborate desserts are worth saving room for.

ripartecafé

mediterranean cuisine + sushi bar
+ music club + exhibition space

via degli orti di trastevere 3 00153 roma t 06 586181
f 065814550 email info@riparte.com www.riparte.cor

Corsetti il Galeone

Piazza San Cosimato 27 (06 580 9009/ www.corsettii galeone.it). Tram to viale Trastevere. **Meals served** noon-3.30pm, 7.30-midnight Mon, Tue, Thur-Sun; 7.30pm-midnight Wed. **Average** €€€. **Credit** AmEx, DC, MC, V. Tucked away in one of Trastevere's quieter piazze, this old-fashioned fish restaurant offers fresh fare cooked in a style as classic as its wood-panelled galleon decor that contrasts with the elevated prices, which have kept pace with the times. The tagliolini with courgette flowers and scampi are among standout primi, while the mixed shellfish grill and sea bream baked in a salt crust are as delicate as they come. Lobsters are fished straight from the tank in the entrance. The wine list is solid, if uninspired. The kitsch nautical-themed dining room upstairs makes the place a favourite with tour groups. In summer, the action moves outside, on to pavement tables screened off from the passing traffic by potted shrubs.

Da Enzo

Via dei Vascellari 29 (06 581 8355). Bus to Isola Tiberina. **Meals served** 12.45-3pm, 7.45-11pm Mon-Sat. Closed 2wks Aug. **Average** €-€€. **Credit** AmEx, MC, V. A plain, rustic, unreformed Roman trattoria, with six or seven tables inside and a few more outside on a quiet lane in the southern part of Trastevere, not far from the church of Santa Cecilia. It does decent versions of traditional dishes like penne all'arrabbiata, spaghetti alla carbonara, ossobuco and coda alla vaccinara at very affordable prices. The main drawback is the excruciatingly slow and rather offhand service. Frankly, if you're in a hurry, don't even think of dining here.

Il Boom

Via dei Fienaroli 30A (06 589 7196). Tram to viale Trastevere. **Meals served** 7.30pm-midnight Mon-Sat. Closed 2wks Aug. **Average** €€. **Credit** AmEx, DC, MC, V. There are few themed restaurants in Rome – thank God – but at least Boom does its chosen genre, the 1960s, with a certain verve and charm. Blow-up B&W photos of the post-Dolce Vita years dominate a single white room, with colour provided by Vespa-upholstered chairs. The Calabrian chef lays on a southern Italian bill of fare, with vegetable- and seafood-oriented pasta dishes. The cuisine has its ups and downs; play safe on the secondi by ordering a creative salad such as the finocchio, arance e olive nere (fennel, orange and black olive), and get back on track with the calorific desserts, which include an excellent tiramisù. Perhaps the best thing about the place is the background music: your chance, at last, to hear what 'The House of the Rising Sun' sounds like in Italian.

Trastevere & Monteverde

Il Boom. *See p139.*

La Gensola

Piazza della Gensola 15 (06 583 2758). Tram to viale Trastevere/bus to Isola Tiberina. **Meals served** 12.30-3pm, 7.30pm-midnight Mon-Fri, Sun; 7.30pm-midnight Sat. Closed 2wks Aug. **Average** €€. **Credit** AmEx, DC, MC, V.

Locals fondly recall the days when this place was run by an affable Sicilian with half-moon glasses. The new owners have kept the Sicilian slant but lost much of the atmosphere of that one-man show. But in a Trastevere dominated by cucina romana, La Gensola still offers a valid alternative. To make the most of the menu, stick to the Sicilian specialities, which are marked in bold. The mezzemaniche ai broccoli siciliani (pasta with broccoli and tomato) and the involtini di pesce spada (grilled swordfish parcels filled with anchovies, breadcrumbs, pinenuts and sultanas) are both among the best options among many unique combinations. Sadly, the wine list has few such ambitions. In summer, it's a toss-up between the stuffy interior and the few outside tables, lapped by fragrant gusts of carbon monoxide.

Ostriche a Colazione

Via dei Vascellari 21 (06 589 8896). Tram to viale Trastevere/bus to Isola Tiberina. **Meals served** 8-11pm Mon-Sat. Closed 2wks Aug. **Average** €€€€. **Credit** AmEx, DC, MC V.

Although it's centrally located, this friendly, elegantly feminine seafood oasis tucked away on a quiet Trastevere backstreet is not the kind of place you might expect to easily stumble upon while wandering around Rome. But believe us, it does exist, and it's worth finding. If you track it down, try the plump, briny ostriche (oysters) that give the restaurant its name – though the opening hours preclude ordering them a colazione (for breakfast). Other fresh, simply prepared (though steeply priced) seafood dishes include a salad of rocket, prawns and parmesan, grilled calamari or pesce all'aquapazza (one's choice of fresh fish cooked in 'crazy water' – a lightly spiced fish and tomato broth, stewed with potatoes and cherry tomatoes). The menu leans toward southern Italian specialities, including cannoli (fried pastry cylinders, filled with ricotta and candied fruit).

Pulses and rice spill from jute sacks in Innocenzi (piazza San Cosimato 66), a marvellous old-fashioned grocery.

Paris

Piazza San Calisto 7A (06 581 5378). Tram to viale
Trastevere. **Meals served** 12.30-3pm, 7.45-11pm Tue-
Sat; 12.30-3pm Sun. Closed 3wks Aug. **Average** €€€.
Credit AmEx, DC, MC, V.

Don't be fooled by the name; this upmarket family
restaurant in the heart of Trastevere is adamantly
Roman. This is one of the few places in town where you
can still sample minestra di arzilla ai broccoli (skate soup,
with broccoli and pasta fragments). Paris highlights the
Jewish side of the city's culinary traditions, most
obviously in the wonderful gran fritto vegetale con bacalà
(a fry-up of artichokes, courgettes and their flowers, plus
salt cod). The service is a little slow at times, but
reassuringly old-fashioned, like the decor, with a large
faux-medieval fireplace in the main dining room. In
summer, there are a few tables outside in the square,
which teems with life in the evening.

Riparte Café

Via degli Orti di Trastevere 7 (06 586 1816). Tram
to viale Trastevere. **Meals served** 8pm-2am Tue-Sun.
Closed end July-mid Sept. **Average** €€-€€€.
Credit AmEx, MC, V.

Inside Rome's first boutique hotel sits this large,
minimalist, multi-function café, awash in gallery white
and bright orange. If you can get past the bouncer at the
revolving door – a pretentious and unnecessary detail –
you can tuck into seafood dishes like pappardelle con
frutti di mare e pachino (large noodles with seafood and
cherry tomatoes) and simple fish mains. There is a
separate sushi and sashimi menu and a nice selection of
salads. Riparte is not just a bustling restaurant, but also
a venue for monthly art exhibitions. But perhaps the most
eye-catching objets d'art in this chic eaterie are the diners
fuelling up for Suite, the club-of-the-moment, next door.

Pizzerie

Da Ivo

Via di San Francesco a Ripa 158 (06 581 7082). Tram to
viale Trastevere. **Meals served** 6pm-1am Mon, Tue-Sun.
Closed 1wk Sept. **Average** €. **Credit** AmEx, DC, MC, V.

One of the most famous pizzerie in Rome, as is evident
from the throngs of eager clients waiting in the street.
The seating is extremely squashed, with 200 hungry
souls jammed into a space that would be tight for half
that number, but the atmosphere is electric (especially on
match days), the pizzas acceptable and the service prompt
if inelegant. There's also a decent range of pasta dishes,
for those who dare to go for both icons of popular Italian
cuisine at the same sitting.

Riparte Café

Dar Poeta ★

Vicolo del Bologna 45 (06 588 0516). Bus to piazza
Trilussa. **Meals served** 7.30pm-midnight daily.
Average €. **Credit** AmEx, MC, V.
This bustling pizzeria in the heart of Trastevere uses the
slow-rise method introduced by nouvelle pizza guru
Angelo Iezzi (*see p.206*). Pizzas here have fluffy bases
and creative toppings, including the namesake pizza
(zucchini, sausage and spicy pepper) and the bodrilla
(apples and Grand Marnier). The varied bruschette are
first-rate, and a selection of healthy salads offer a break
from pastry. Try to leave room for dessert, as the sweet
calzone stuffed with nutella and ricotta is to die for. You
can eat late, and the waiters are genuinely friendly, but
be prepared to queue, as they don't take bookings.

Da Vittorio

Via di San Cosimato 14A (06 580 0353). Tram to viale
Trastevere. **Meals served** 7.30pm-midnight Mon-Sat.
Average €. **Credit** MC, V.
Vittorio was here way before Neapolitan pizzas became
trendy, and no doubt it will be when the fad has passed.
He's as napoletano as they come, and so are his pizzas,
like the self-celebratory Vittorio (mozzarella, parmesan,
fresh tomato and basil). The place is minute, but bursts
with exuberance.

RESTAURANT AI FIENAROLI

Italian chef Nicola Cavallaro is taking Rome by storm...one plate at a time. Young and dynamic, this world traveller has mastered the art of fusion while maintaining his classical Italian roots, resulting in an artful and delicious mix of world cuisine that inspires even traditional Italians to flock to his restaurant every night.

VIA DEI FIENAROLI, 5 - 00153 ROMA
Tel. 06.5884474

The best fish

Alberto Ciarla
See p134.

La Rosetta
See p60.

Quinzi e Gabrieli
See p65.

Sangallo
See p67.

Fauro
See p194.

Panattoni – I Marmi
Viale Trastevere 53 (06 580 0919). Tram to viale Trastevere. **Meals served** 6.30pm-2am Mon, Tue, Thur-Sun. Closed 3wks Aug. **Average** €. **No credit cards**.
Better known as l'obitorio (the morgue) on account of its marble slab tables; there's nothing deathly about Panattoni, one of the liveliest (and cheapest) pizzerie in Trastevere. In summer the pavement outside fills up with tables and you can dine to the spectacle of the new super-trams gliding along viale Trastevere. The pizzas, though, are not the best in Rome, and service can be ruthless.

International

ATM Sushi Bar
Via della Pentinenza 7 (06 6830 7053). Bus to ponte Mazzini or ponte Sisto. **Meals served** 8pm-midnight Tue-Sun. Closed Aug. **Average** €€-€€€. **Credit** AmEx, MC, V.
Italian sushi can be criminally bad; maybe that's why ATM is located just around the corner from the neighbourhood prison. But in reality, this Roman offshoot of a trendy Milanese bar-restaurant is a cut above the limp seaweed brigade. The decor is full-out industrial chic with tin ceilings, rusted iron beams and black leather sofas. The miso soup and tempura are solid starters, the sashimi and sushi fresh and tasty. The California rolls go off the rails, though, by hurling radicchio, tomatoes, mayonnaise and salmon into the (strange) mix. Shortcomings – such as the limited menu and the elevated prices – are made up for by the illicit thrill of being a million miles from a plate of carbonara.

Thai Inn

Bali Pub

Via del Mattonato 29 (06 589 6089). Bus to ponte Sisto.
Meals served 9.30pm-3am Tue-Sun. Closed mid July-end
Aug. **Average** €€. **Credit** AmEx, MC, V.
This Indonesian oasis has expanded and is now two bars
in one. Upon entering, you are immediately thrust into a
shadowy, exotic enclave of bamboo, tapestry and
candlelight. The cushioned booths and sofas with tables
are all about 10 inches above floor level – perfect for a
romantic encounter over a relaxing fruit cocktail or
Indonesian tea. In the larger but less atmospheric back
rooms one can select from a limited Asian menu, where
Indonesian dishes like chicken satay and roast pork in
kecap manis (a sweet, thicker soy sauce) are more
interesting than sushi and tempura.

Jaipur

*Via di San Francesco a Ripa 56 (06 580 3992). Tram to
viale Trastevere.* **Meals served** 7pm-midnight Mon;
noon-3pm, 7pm-midnight Tue-Sun. **Average** €-€€.
Credit MC, V.

The food is delicious, the staff courteous, and nothing on the menu exceeds €12. This should help you overlook the carabinieri-interrogation-room lighting and garish sunflower colour scheme of one of Rome's newest Indian restaurants. The menu is extensive, from the basic starters to the large selection of tandoori specials, curries and murghs (the murgh maccan, charcoal-grilled chicken with a butter-tomato gravy, is particularly tasty). There are two pages of vegetarian dishes, including a baighan bharta (aubergine purée cooked in a clay oven, dressed with spices) so good it makes you want to lick the earthenware bowl. Add to this a good dessert menu, and you have one of the best bargains in Trastevere.

Thai Inn

Via Federico Ozanam 94 (06 582 03 145). Bus to via Ozanam/tram to piazza San Giovanni di Dio. **Meals served** 6-11.30pm Tue-Fri; 12.30-2.30pm, 6-11.30pm Sat, Sun. **Average** €€. **Credit** AmEx, DC, MC, V.
The menu announces authentic Asean (Association of South-east Asian Nations) cuisine, but you only get three of the ten member countries: Thailand, Malaysia and Indonesia. This, however, is no disappointment. The owner, Heng, imports fresh lemongrass, curry and lime leaf, which accounts for the rich flavours of his vast menu (order by number). Tried and true are the spicy beef salad, the even spicier tia yam gung soup and the monumental mi goreng Petronas twin towers. Most of the menu is well translated, except for the charming but slightly confusing 'fried fat rice noodle with tree delicious'. Of the two dining rooms, the back garden room is the more intimate one, with its lush bamboo greenery, kitschy art and soundtrack of cheery Thai pop.

Wine bars & pubs

Artù

Largo MD Fumasoni Biondi 5 (06 588 0398). Bus to piazza Trilussa. **Meals served** 6pm-2am Tue-Sun. Closed 3wks Aug. **Credit** MC, V.
This friendly place in a little square that is an extension of piazza Sant'Egidio hovers somewhere between being an Italian bar and an English pub. The stained-glass windows, selection of high-quality brews, polished wood bar and smattering of English-speaking regulars lean towards Albion; while the wine list, fashion TV and aperitivo buffet (nightly from 6.30pm to 9pm) are reminders that we're still in bella Italia. There's also a full menu of pub fare, with sandwiches (try the Sir Lucas, which features sausage, fontina cheese and pink sauce),

Da Ivo. *See p142.*

along with pasta dishes and meat courses. This is also a
very handy spot for a pre- or post-film nibble and drink,
as it's just around the corner from the popular Pasquino
English-language cinema.

Enoteca Ferrara

*Via del Moro 1A (06 5833 3920). Tram to viale
Trastevere/bus to piazza Trilussa.* **Open** *Oct-Apr* 10am-
2am Mon, Wed-Sun. *May-Sept* noon-2am Mon, Wed-Sun.
Meals served 12.30-4pm, 7.30-11.30pm. **Credit** DC, MC, V.
In a surprisingly large space for Trastevere, the Paolillo
sisters run a tasteful imbibery with a well-stocked, 850-
label cellar. The apartheid wine lists (one book for whites,
another for reds) provide a happy evening's reading. The
serious eater, however, books in advance and takes
advantage of the restaurant's inventive offerings like
zuppetta di cozze e vongole (mussel and clam soup) and
filetto di persico fritto (fried fillet of perch, served with
red cabbage and lemon). On most days there is also a set
menu (€55, excluding wine). Otherwise, expect to spend
around €10 for a glass of wine and a snack, €40 for a full
meal. From May to September you can wine and dine in
a pretty, quiet garden at the back.

Sisini (via San
Francesco a
Ripa 137) is
Trastevere's
best takeaway
pizza outlet:
the mozzarella
& mushroom
version is
particularly
fine.

Enoteca Trastevere

Via della Lungaretta 86 (06 588 5659). Tram to viale Trastevere. **Meals served** 5pm-2am Mon-Sat; 4pm-1am Sun. Closed 3wks Jan. **Credit** AmEx, MC, V.

The usual enoteca decor prevails at this neighbourhood favourite: wooden tables and chairs, walls lined with hundreds of bottles of mostly Italian wine, and a menu that takes in an assortment of salami and cheeses, bruschette and crostini, salads and desserts. But this enoteca has a couple of less obvious selling points: a large selection of grappas, distilled liquors and amaros by the glass, at reasonable prices; and a good selection of organic wines. The staff are friendly, and there is usually live music at weekends.

Il Cantiniere di Santa Dorotea

Via di Santa Dorotea 9 (06 581 9025/www.ilcant iniere.com). Bus to ponte Sisto. **Meals served** 7pm-2am Mon-Sat. Closed 2wks Aug. **Credit** AmEx, DC, MC, V.

This wine bar has hundreds of vintages and labels and a knowledgeable staff. The owner, Alberto Costantini, maintains a website (www.theworldwineweb.net) and

newsletter for anyone interested in the latest on the
international wine scene. That said, the atmosphere here
is somewhat stifling: the tables are uncomfortable and
the lighting dreary. Outside tables in summer are a safer
bet. The small menu aims high, but salads and daily
specials that yearn to be innovative don't quite achieve
their goal. Stick to the basics – cheese and salamis – and
order a bottle from the extensive wine list, or a glass from
the ample daily selection.

Bars & cafés

Bar Gianicolo

Piazzale Aurelio 5 (06 580 6275). Bus to via Carini.
Open 6am-1am Tue-Sun. **No credit cards.**
Wooden panels and benches lend this tiny bar on the
Gianicolo hill – the site of Garibaldi's doomed battle with
the French – an intimate, chatty feel unusual in Rome.
Fresh carrots and apples juiced on the spot, a range of
exotic sandwiches and light meals and the outside tables
overlooking the Porta di San Pancrazio city gate make it
a good spot for a drink, a snack or lunch after a walk on
the Gianicolo or in nearby Villa Pamphili.

Bar San Calisto

Piazza San Calisto 3/4 (no phone). Tram to
viale Trastevere. **Open** 6am-1.30am Mon-Sat.
No credit cards.
Tourists pay through the nose for coffee or beer in piazza
Santa Maria in Trastevere; locals head for this
unreconstructed bar, known locally as Marcello's, in the
less scenic, but more authentic, adjoining square.
Unassuming and incredibly cheap, it's the haunt of arty
and fringe types (along with a few questionable
characters after sundown) usually seen downing Peroni
beers straight from the bottle or dipping into an affogato
(ice-cream swamped with liqueur).

Della Scala

Via della Scala 4 (06 580 3610). Bus to piazza Trilussa.
Open 4pm-2am daily. **No credit cards.**
Since Trastevere has become such a popular part of town,
business has picked up at this unassuming bar, whose
distinguishing feature is that it has no distinguishing
features. The usual music is played, the usual drinks are
served, the usual bar nibbles offered. But prices are fair,
there is a decent selection of beers and ten or so fruit-
flavored vodkas. This is a good, central spot to head
toward when other bars nearby are packed; and there are
a few pleasant outdoor tables for summertime.

Beyond Frascati

The wines of the Lazio region (of which Rome is the capital) have traditionally been looked down upon – not without justification – as low-grade fuel for the city's numerous osterie and trattorie. The local wine industry centres on the rolling, villa-strewn hills of the Castelli Romani east of the city, around the towns of Frascati and Marino. Its preference for quantity over quality long acted as a brake on the development of a serious regional wine culture. It has to be said, though, that the poor reputation of wine from the Castelli has also historically been the fault of crafty Roman innkeepers and restaurateurs, who would cut good Frascati with cheap Sicilian white to produce a cloudy, urine-coloured brew that at its best could be described as 'onesto' and at its worst was a handy paint-stripper substitute.

Things have changed, though, as Lazio responds to the general Italian demand for quality wine (see p20 **The rise and rise of Italian wine**). The Frascati area still has a small army of farmer-winemakers, who hang a vine branch over the cellar door to show that the new wine is ready to drink straight from the barrel. It also has some more serious players, ranging from huge industrial wineries in the Fontana Candida mould to medium-scale family estates like Di Mauro, Villa Simone and Castel De Paolis, which have started producing wines of some stature. Fontana Candida's Santa Teresa cru is a model of the new clean, lean style of Frascati, while Villa Simone's Vigneto Filonardi offers a more traditional approach, with a flavour that is full, fruity and just slightly abboccato (tending to sweet).

But compared to the pace of the quality wine explosion further south in Campania or Puglia, things are still moving slowly in Lazio. Perhaps the most interesting developments come from the far north of the region, on the shores of Lake Bolsena, where a single producer, Falesco, has overturned the strictly-for-tourists reputation of the curiously named Est! Est!! Est!!! and turned it into an eminently quaffable white that reaches levels of true finesse in the single-vineyard cru Poggio dei Gelsi. Falesco produces a Merlot-based red, Montiano, which has earned a place among the great Italian reds. It also has the distinction of being much cheaper than many of its rivals. In Falesco's wake, other producers in the same area – from Sergio Mottura to Roberto Trappolini – are achieving good results.

In the south of the region there is less to discover, although you'll find the occasional oasis in the wine desert, such as the small but interesting Colle San Lorenzo winery in Cori.

Trastevere & Monteverde

Di Marzio

Piazza Santa Maria in Trastevere 15 (06 581 6095).
Tram to viale Trastevere. **Open** 7am-1am daily.
Credit MC, V.

Piazza Santa Maria is not the cheapest place in Rome to
have a drink, but if you want to admire the fountain and
the church with a drink in your hand, Di Marzio has the
least smarmy service in the square, and the best view.

Friends Art Café

Piazza Trilussa 34 (06 581 6111). Bus to piazza Trilussa.
Open 7am-1.30am Mon-Sat; 6pm-1.30am Sun. Closed 1wk
Aug. **Credit** AmEx, DC, MC, V.

This spruce, modern bar on a corner of piazza Trilussa
has become a popular meeting place for everything from
a morning cornetto and cappuccino to an after-dinner
cocktail. The chrome detailing and brightly coloured

Valzani (via
del Moro 37B)
makes
traditional
Roman
sweets
including
pangiallo and
cioccolato
all'arancia
(chocolate
orange).

plastic chairs in the dining room, coupled with the constant din of fashion TV in the background, lend the place a retro-1980s funhouse feel. Lunch and dinner menus offer the usual suspects (bruschette, salads, pasta dishes) at reasonable prices.

I Dolci di Checco er Carettiere

Via Benedetta 7 (06 5811 413). Bus to Ponte Sisto. **Open** 6.30am-2am Tue-Sun. **No credit cards.**

This small bar behind piazza Trilussa is annexed to one of Trastevere's oldest restaurants – Checco er Carettiere (*see p136*) – but this little version is worth a visit in its own right. It is known for its outstanding cakes and pastries, fresh quiche, crisp crocchette and, most days, tasty baked pasta. For those who are more thirsty than hungry, it also offers a savvy selection of malt whiskies and some of the best gelato this side of the Tiber.

Friends Art Café

Il Giardino dei Ciliegi

Via dei Fienaroli 4 (06 580 3423). Bus/tram to viale Trastevere. **Open** 5pm-1am daily. Closed July-mid Sept. **No credit cards**.

This relaxed and friendly bar with a vaguely 1960s feel is one of the few Roman points of reference for serious tea drinkers. It has dozens of different kinds of tea, from staunch lapsang souchong to flighty herbal infusions. Freshly baked cakes, biscuits and buttered toast continue the five o'clock theme; and there are also a few salads and other savoury snacks on offer.

Ombre Rosse ★

Piazza Sant'Egidio 12 (06 588 415). Bus to piazza Trilussa. **Open** 8am-2am Mon-Sat; 6pm-2am Sun. Closed 1wk Aug. **Credit** AmEx, MC, V.

In the heart of Trastevere on a scenic piazza, this café is a central meeting spot day and night. Its continuous hours of operation are a plus, making it perfect for a morning coffee, a late lunch or a light dinner (try the chicken salad or fresh soups; allow €15 for a light meal). It reaches capacity pre- and post-dinner, when snagging one of the coveted outdoor tables is quite a coup. Service is slow but friendly, so as the bartender crushes the ice for your next caiparoska, you have plenty of time to watch the Trasteverine menagerie go by.

Sacchetti ★

Piazza San Cosimato 61/62 (06 581 5374). Tram to viale Trastevere. **Open** Oct-Apr 5.30am-10pm Tue-Sun. May-Sept 5.30am-midnight Tue-Sun. **No credit cards**.

The Sacchetti family runs one of the least touristy bars in Trastevere, with tables outside all year round and a big tearoom upstairs. Everything is made in-house; the cornetti and the ricotta-filled sfogliatelle romane are memorable. The ice-creams, hidden behind the bar in old-fashioned steel barrels, are delicious too. The shutters stay up until around 1am on hot summer evenings.

Stardust

Vicolo de' Renzi, 4 (06 583 20 875). Bus to piazza Trilussa. **Open** 7pm-2am Mon; 7.30pm-2am Tue-Sat; noon-2am Sun. **No credit cards**.

This tiny space with a handful of tables, chairs and cushioned benches lining the walls has become an institution for local night owls. Before dinner, the place has a lounge atmosphere, perfect for an aperitivo and a languid chat. After dinner, it undergoes a metamorphosis, becoming a raucous, smoky pub where the bartenders blast anything from Lenny Kravitz to Cuban jazz, Czech polkas to opera. The crowd is a colourful mix of local denizens, out-of-work actors and expats, and crowd watching is one of the best pastimes here.

Aventine
& Testaccio

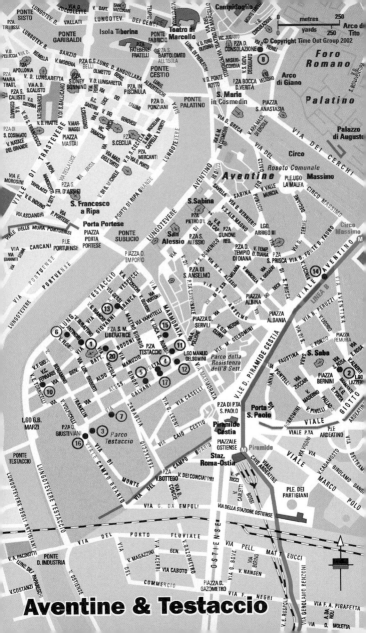

Aventine & Testaccio

Testaccio is one of the few areas of central Rome where a sense of community is still strongly felt, and where the line between courtyard and street is blurred enough to allow old ladies to pop into the local alimentari in their dressing gown and slippers. Built as a low-rent worker's suburb at the beginning of the 20th century, it has recently become one of the main poles of Roman nightlife. The restaurants specialise in affordable, down-home Roman cooking, a vocation encouraged by the proximity of the municipal slaughterhouse, which shut in the 1970s. Today, though, a new breed of creative trattorie make Testaccio one of the best quartieri in Rome for low-cost, high-quality dining.

Testaccio market

Restaurants

Agustarello ★

Via Giovanni Branca 100 (06 574 6585). Bus to via Marmorata/piazza Santa Maria Liberatrice. **Meals served** 12.30-3pm, 7.30-11.30pm Mon-Sat. Closed 3wks Aug. **Average €€. No credit cards**.

The decor in this trattoria couldn't be more basic, but what matters here is respect for the Roman tradition in all its anatomical detail. Dishes such as rigatoni con la pajata (pasta with baby veal intestines) were briefly rocked by the BSE scare, but are now defiantly centre stage on the menu again; if you prefer to play safe, the tonnarelli cacio e pepe (with sheep's cheese and black pepper) are equally fine. Agustarello's flagship secondo is the succulent involtini con il sedano (veal rolls with celery stuffing).

Al Callarello

Via Salvator Rosa 8 (06 574 7575). Metro Circo Massimo/bus/tram to viale Aventino. **Meals served** noon-3pm, 7.30-11pm Mon-Sat. Closed 2wks Aug. **Average €€. Credit** MC, V.

Gastronomic temple it ain't; but the Callarello still has a lot going for it. First, the setting, in a pretty square off the main tourist track on the hill of San Saba. Second, the tables that spill out over the pavement in summer, expanding and contracting to keep up with the demand. And third, the wood-oven pizzas, which offer diners a valid evening alternative to a competent but unexciting fish- or meat-based menu. If everyone around you seems to be speaking a different language, that's because the FAO – the UN food agency – is just around the corner.

Checchino dal 1887 ★

Via di Monte Testaccio 30 (06 574 6318). Bus/tram to via Marmorata/bus to via Galvani. **Meals served** 12.30-3pm, 8pm-midnight Tue-Sat. Closed Aug. **Average €€€€. Credit** AmEx, DC, MC, V.

Nestling among the trendy bars and clubs opposite Testaccio's former slaughterhouse, the Mariani family's historic restaurant is Rome's leading temple of authentic cucina romana. The cellar at Checchino dal 1887 feeds one of the most extensive wine lists in Rome. Specialities include trippa (tripe), pajata (baby lamb intestines full of mother's milk) and coda alla vaccinara (braised oxtail). If you're feeling gutsy, go for the bollito misto (mixed boiled meats) and play guess-that-gelatinous-substance. Desserts are less extreme, and feature, among their other charms, a delicious stracciatella (ricotta, almond and chocolate chip) cake.

Ketumbar. *See p161.*

Rome's best-stocked deli, Volpetti (via Marmorata 47/www.volpetti.com) has a huge range of Italian cheeses and salami, plus high-quality pasta, olive oil and other gourmet treats.

Da Felice

Via Mastro Giorgio 29 (06 574 6800). Metro Piramide/ bus/tram to via Marmorata. **Meals served** 12.15-2.30pm, 8-10.30pm Mon-Sat. Closed Aug. **Average** €. **No credit cards**.

The thrill of this neighbourhood trat is not so much the food – good, traditional Roman cooking with lots of offal – as trying to get in. The inaptly named Felice – not happy at all, but a morose septuagenarian – covers every table in 'riservato' signs before he opens for the day, just so that he can announce 'no room' Mad Hatter style to anyone he doesn't fancy. It helps if you come on like a trader from nearby Testaccio market: jeans, stained T-shirt, broad Roman dialect. Once in, order the classic bucatini all'amatriciana followed by fagioli con le cotiche (beans with pork rind), and bask in the satisfaction of being among the chosen few.

Da Oio a Casa Mia

Via Galvani 43/45 (06 578 2680). Metro Piramide/ bus/tram to Via Marmorata. **Meals served** 12.30-3pm, 7.30-11pm Mon-Sat. Closed 2wks Aug. **Average** €€. **Credit** AmEx, MC, V.

On the edge of Testaccio, hard by the Protestant Cemetery, this honest trattoria di quartiere is low on pretensions and high on old-fashioned elbow-to-elbow

atmosphere. The food and clientele are resolutely Roman, with the accent on primi like tonnarelli alla gricia (with bacon and pecorino cheese) and pasta e ceci (with chickpeas). The main courses fall a notch below the excellent primi, and the desserts are nothing to write home about, but it's always packed, so come early, or book. In summer, tables crowd the pavement outside.

Il Piccolo Alpino

Via Orazio Antinori 5 (06 574 1386). Bus to via Rubattino. **Meals served** 12.30-2.30pm, 6-11pm Tue-Sun. **Average €. No credit cards**.

This ultra-cheap, no-frills pizzeria-trattoria in a residential Testaccio sidestreet is about as far as you can get from the tourist herd without leaving the Centro Storico. There's a telly in the corner (with football on Sunday evenings), beer on tap and rough Castelli Romani wine in the fridge; but the pizzas are good, and the pasta too, as long as you stick to the house specialities: spaghetti con le vongole (with clams) and penne all'arrabbiata (in tomato and chilli sauce). In summer, tables invade the road, kids play tag among the cars, and it all feels like a scene from Fellini's Roma.

Ketumbar

Via Galvani 24 (06 5730 5338). Bus/tram to via Marmorata/ bus to via Galvani. **Meals served** 8pm-midnight daily. Closed Aug. **Average €€€. Credit** AmEx, DC, MC, V.

There's an odd culture clash in this brand new, hyper-trendy club-restaurant. The setting couldn't be more Roman, in one of the old wine cellars that burrow into Monte Testaccio. But the decor is modern, chill-out ethnic, from the lacquered chests to the staff uniforms to the paper-lantern wall lights. Oddly, it works – as does the fusion fare, which mixes oriental and Italian ingredients, as in a mango salad with bottarga di muggine (mullet roe). You can also down a plate of pasta and a glass of wine in the bar, which stays open until around 2am. The only duff note is the resident DJ who cranks up the music so loud that you can't hear yourself eat, let alone speak.

La Torricella

Via E Torricelli 2/4 (06 574 6311/www.la-torricella.com). Bus to lungotevere Testaccio. **Meals served** noon-3.30pm, 7pm-midnight daily. **Average €€. Credit** AmEx, DC, MC, V.

For the full experience, come to La Torricella in the summer and sit at one of the outside tables in this residential street. Babies cry, families fight and on match nights a hundred televisions provide a wall-of-sound accompaniment to your meal. Inside, the spirit of one of actor-director Roberto Benigni's favourite haunts comes through. The food consists of good-value

Roman with a fishy angle: the spaghetti alla vongole (with clams) is always reliable. In the evening, there are an array of pizzas also on offer.

Luna Piena ★

Via Luca della Robbia 15/17 (06 575 0279). Metro Piramide/bus to via Marmorata. **Meals served** 7.30-11.30pm Mon-Sat; 12.30-3pm, 7.30-11.30pm Sun. Closed mid June-mid July. **Average** €€. **Credit** AmEx, DC, MC, V.

This local trattoria with updated, artsy decor serves a good range of culinary classics. Traditionalists will be satisfied by the hard-to-beat bucatini alla gricia (pasta in a bacon and pecorino sauce) and the saltimbocca (veal with ham and sage), while the more adventurous might opt for the own-made ravioli di zucca (with pumpkin) or the southern Italian dish of crema di fave con cicoria (broad bean purée served with wild chicory). Keep an eye out for the day's specials chalked up on a board at the door. Although space is rather cramped, the wallet-friendly bill makes Luna Piena one of the best value for money experiences in Rome.

Tuttifrutti ★

Via Luca della Robbia 3A (06 575 7902). Metro Piramide/bus/tram to via Marmorata. **Meals served** 8-11pm Tue-Sun. Closed Aug. **Average** €€. **Credit** AmEx, MC, V.

Behind an anonymous frosted glass door, this 'circolo culturale' is actually one of Testaccio's best-value dining

Passi (via Mastro Giorgio 87) is a real neighbourhood bakery. Queue three deep with the old ladies for oven-hot pizza bianca, served by a crew of fast-talking, Lazio-supporting doughboys.

The offal truth

The unspeakable parts of the beast have long been a major component of the Roman culinary tradition. A hundred years ago, the so-called quinto quarto, or 'fifth quarter', of tripe, tail, intestines and so on, went by right to the workers of the municipal slaughterhouse in Testaccio. Thus it was in the humble trattorie of that neighbourhood that inventive cooks learnt to put the workers' offcuts to good use.

It was a cook named Sora Ferminia who came up with the recipe for coda alla vaccinara – literally, 'tail in the style of the slaughterhouse worker'. The popularity of this dish – in which an oxtail is braised in a celery broth – soon led to a veritable run on tails at local butchers.

The other classic Roman offal dish is that vegetarian favourite, rigatoni alla pajata – pajata being the abomasum – or fourth stomach – of a baby calf, and the passage leading thereto. When the calf is slaughtered young enough,

L'Oasi della Birra. *See p165.*

this passage is still filled with curdled maternal milk – hence the part's American name, marrow gut (an essential ingredient of a cowboy dish known as 'sonofabitch stew'). The pajata is cooked in lard, onion, celery and parsley, and served with rigatoni.

Other favourite quinto quarto specialities include fagioli con le cotiche (beans with pork scratchings); insalata di zampi (hoof jelly salad); and animelle (sweetbread – the spongy white pancreas and thymus glands,

generally served fried). Tripe (trippa) is also big in Rome; other bits of the animal you may see on the menu or somewhere near it include cervello (brain), lingua (tongue), guanciale (pig's cheek, cured in salt and pepper) and nervetti (strips of cartilage).

Buon appetito!

To get in touch with your innards self, head for one of the two Testaccio temples of cucina romana, **Checchino dal 1887** and **Agustarello** (*see p158* for both).

experiences – on a par with **Luna Piena** (*see p162*). Once past the free 'membership card' formality (it's a licensing law thing, apparently), you can concentrate on the daily changing menu of creative pan-Italian fare that might include an antipasto of pecorino di fossa (a cheese from the Marches) with honey and pears, followed by tonnarelli con cicoria e rosmarino (with dandelion leaves and rosemary) and agnello al forno con patate (baked lamb with potatoes). You'll be talked through the choices by the earnest, welcoming young crew running the place.

Pizzerie

Remo ★

Piazza Santa Maria Liberatrice 44 (06 574 6270).
Bus/tram to via Marmorata/bus to piazza Santa Maria
Liberatrice. **Meals served** 7pm-12.30am Mon-Sat. Closed
Aug. **Average** €. **No credit cards**.
The best place in town for authentic pizza romana, this is a Testaccio institution, with a prime location on the district's main piazza. You can sit at wonky tables balanced on the pavement, or in the cavernous interior, overseen by Lazio team photos. The bruschette al pomodoro are the finest in Rome.

International

Court Delicati

Viale Aventino 39 (06 574 6108). Metro Circo
Massimo/bus/tram to viale Aventino. **Meals served**
noon-2.45pm, 7.30-11pm Tue-Sun. Closed Aug.
Average €€. **Credit** AmEx, DC, MC, V.

The best **cucina romana**

Checchino dal 1887
See p159.

Paris
See p142.

Agustarello
See p158.

Zampagna
See p208.

Osteria dell'Angelo
See p128.

Bar del Mattatoio. *See p166.*

Court Delicati is basically a decent Chinese restaurant, but it has gained renown as one of the few places to add Thai and Indonesian dishes to the usual repertoire. So as well as better-than-average steamed dumplings and hot crispy beef, regulars can also enjoy violently spicy tom yam soup and a very passable nasi goreng. Beer and wine are as reasonably priced as everything else on the menu. Very popular with staff from the nearby UN food agency at lunch, and with largish groups of adventurous Italians in the evenings.

Wine bars & pubs

L'Oasi della Birra ★
Piazza Testaccio 41 (06 574 6122). Bus or tram to via Marmorata. **Meals served** 7.30pm-1am Mon-Sat. Closed 2wks Aug. **Average** €€. **Credit** MC, V.
In the basement of a modest enoteca on Testaccio's market square, this 'Oasis of Beer' has over 500 brews on offer. It's one of few places in Rome where you can track down the products of Italian microbreweries such as the award-winning Menabrea, and the selection of wines by the bottle is almost equally impressive. The food ranges from snacks (crostini, bruschette) to full-scale meals with a Teutonic-Magyar slant (goulash, wurstel, krauti). Booking is a good idea, although the ten outside tables operate year round, weather permitting.

Aventine & Testaccio

Court Delicati. *See p164.*

Bars & cafés

Bar del Mattatoio
Piazza O Giustiniani 3 (06 574 6017). Bus to via Galvani.
Open 6am-9pm Mon-Sat. **No credit cards.**
A charming brick doll's house of a bar, with Gothic
recesses in the front. One of the earliest-opening bars in
Rome, it once catered for the meatworkers from the
municipal slaughterhouse opposite; nowadays the Tozzi
family serve ancient locals and dawn revellers from
Testaccio clubland.

Il Seme e la Foglia
*Via Galvani 18 (06 574 3008). Bus/tram to via Marmorata/
bus to via Galvani.* **Open** 7.45am-1.30am Mon-Sat; 6pm-
1.30am Sun. Closed 3wks Aug. **No credit cards.**
Once a po-faced macrobiotic affair, this corner bar has
become a lively daytime snack bar and evening pre-club
stop; it's especially favoured by musicians from the nearby
Scuola Popolare di Musica. At midday there's always a
pasta dish, plus creative salads and exotic filled rolls.

Linari ★
*Via Zabaglia 9A/B (06 578 2358). Bus to piazza Santa
Maria Liberatrice.* **Open** 7am-10.30pm Mon, Wed-Sun.
No credit cards.
A classic Testaccio bar-pasticceria, run by a large family
(in both senses of the adjective). The freshly baked cornetti
draw such a large crowd of locals in the morning that it's
often three deep at the bar. There are a few tables outside
for those who want to take time out to observe this most
Roman of neighbourhoods over a cappuccino.

Monti, Termini & San Giovanni

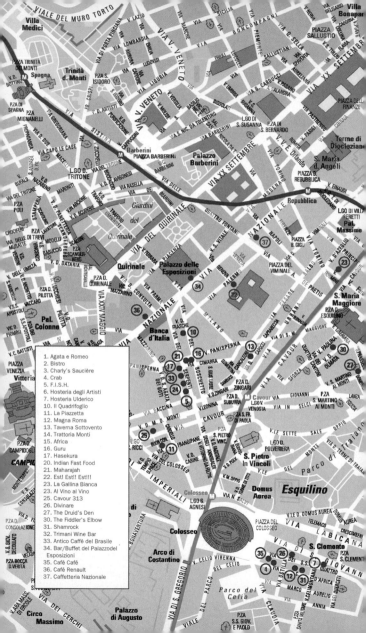

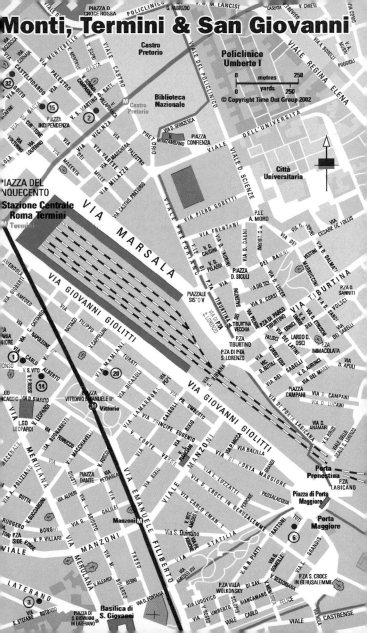

Made up of three distinct quartieri, the south-eastern quadrant of the Centro Storico is an area of contrasts. The rione (ward) of Monti stretches from the tight cluster of medieval streets east of the Forum – once the Suburra, ancient Rome's biggest slum – to the long Risorgimento avenues of the Esquilino, around Stazione Termini. Now a mecca for Rome's African and Asian communities, the area around piazza Vittorio was once covered in vast orchards and patrician villas. Just to the east of the Colosseum, the small Celio enclave has a villagey atmosphere. Further south and east lies San Giovanni, an area of post-Unification apartment blocks that has sprung up around the basilica of the same name. This is not one of the culinary hubs of Rome, and the area around the station in particular teems with the lowest forms of gastronomic life. But there are some diamonds hidden in the rough, if you know where to look. This is also one of the few parts of the city with a decent selection of international restaurants – especially South Asian and East African.

Restaurants

Agata e Romeo ★
Via Carlo Alberto 45 (06 446 6115). Metro Vittorio/bus to Santa Maria Maggiore. **Meals served** 1-2.30pm, 8-11pm Mon-Fri. Closed 2wks Aug, 2wks Jan. **Average** €€€€. **Credit** AmEx, DC, MC, V.
It may be slightly off the beaten track, in the shadows of Santa Maria Maggiore, but this intimate cordon bleu haven is well worth seeking out. It's a family affair, with husband Romeo presiding over the dining room (and the extensive wine list), while wife Agata elevates traditional Roman cuisine to a new level. She takes pleasure in simplicity, as in the amuse-gueule of lightly fried shrimp and baby calamari with white beans. The antipasto of budino di cipolla con scaloppa di fegato grasso d'oca

(onion pudding with foie gras) comes in a sauce of fragrant dessert wine. Among the primi, the cannelloni filled with a white duck ragu are memorable. The coda di bue con crema di sedano rapa (terrine of oxtail stew with cream of celeriac) elates both the meat-and-potatoes lover and gourmand. The dessert list includes a chocolate triple-whammy of semi-sweet chocolate cake with chocolate sorbet and chocolate semifreddo. Because of all this, it is unsurprising that this place is often packed, and thus booking is a good idea.

Bistro

Via Palestro 40 (06 4470 2868). Metro Castro Pretorio/ bus to piazza Indipendenza. **Meals served** noon-3pm, 7pm-midnight Mon-Fri; 7pm-midnight Sat. Closed 3wks Aug. **Average** €€. **Credit** AmEx, DC, MC, V.

A recent addition to Rome's growing army of restaurant-wine bars, this is where art nouveau meets classical Rome. Airy, arched ceilings decorated with whimsical wrought-iron chandeliers and golden mirrors create a rich, playful atmosphere. Unlike standard Roman wine bars with their platters of cold cuts, Bistro has an original lunch and dinner menu. Chef Emanuele Vizzini's fusion approach is exemplified by his fettuccine al Cabernet con scampi (with prawns and vegetables in a red wine sauce) or the so-called 'Nasdaq tagliolini' with lobster (the US-dollar-green pasta gets its colour from curaçao liqueur). The well-stocked cellar holds 300 lesser known, high-quality wines, 12 of which are available by the glass. The place always tends to warm up late in the evening, when one of the young owners usually cranks up the music for those in search of a late night party.

 The best creative trattoria

Al Ponte della Ranocchia
See p202.

Matricianella
See p38.

Il Dito e la Luna
See p200.

Tuttifrutti
See p161.

Ditirambo
See p89.

Monti, Termini & San Giovanni

Crab

*Via Capo d'Africa 2 (06 7720 3636). Metro Colosseo
or bus/tram to Colosseo.* **Meals served** 8-11.30pm Mon;
1-3pm, 8-11.30pm Tue-Sat. Closed 3wks Aug, 2wks Dec,
Jan. **Average** €€€. **Credit** AmEx, DC, MC, V.
Oyster lovers swear it's one of the only places in Rome
to get them really fresh. Tucked down a side street near
the Colosseum, this rather anonymous restaurant offers
a vast range of seafood, including the eponymous crab
(granchio), scallops (capesante) and spiny lobster
(aragosta) – the latter fished fresh from the large tank
that dominates the entrance. Don't even think of ordering
a steak, or even a sea bass: it's strictly crustaceans and
molluscs here. The kitchen's Sardinian leanings are
exemplified in dishes such as the ravioli di astice (lobster
ravioli), a succulent gnocchi con vongole e cozze (with

Hosteria degli Artisti. *See p177.*

small clams and mussels), and the second course tegamino di calamari con patate in forma (baked squid with potatoes). The wine selection here is quite good, oysters come on a ceremonial four-tiered serving dish and the big hot or cold combination plates look like something out of *The Little Mermaid*.

F.I.S.H.

Via dei Serpenti 16 (06 4782 4962). Metro Cavour/bus to via Nazionale. **Meals served** 8pm-midnight Tue-Sun. Closed 2wks Aug. **Average** €€. **Credit** AmEx, MC, V.
The latest fusion eaterie to open in a city that has gone from zero to 'sushi overload' in less than three years. But F.I.S.H. (Fine International Seafood House) at least has the right credentials, with Italo-Australian owner brothers and a Japanese-Brazilian sushi chef. Pale slatted

Magna Roma

It was only a matter of time before Rome got its first ancient Roman restaurant, or thermopolium. But this is no tourist toga party: Magna Roma ('Greater Rome', but also – in modern Roman dialect – 'eat Rome') takes its task extremely seriously: there is even an archaeologist on hand to talk you through your meal. The experience doesn't come cheap, but for those with a real interest in ancient Rome, it provides a rare chance to eat and drink some classical culture.

Just along the road from the Colosseum, the restaurant is done out as a rather more

refined version of an inn from the second century AD, with marble counter at the entrance, undulating brick-vaulted ceiling and reproductions of food-themed classical murals.

At dinner (8.30-11.30pm), guests are greeted by owner Luciano Marino (who speaks fluent English) and by the archaeologist Franco Nicastro, who deliver an introduction to the meal while damsels in early 1970s-style togas hand out beakers of muslum (grape must, sweetened with honey) and offer a selection of appetisers including quails' eggs, moretum (which are small cakes of cheese, garlic and herbs), lupins, nuts, olives and so forth.

These tasters are followed by a fixed (but seasonally changing) succession of dishes, such as lenticulam de castaineis (an intriguing lentil and chestnut soup), minutal dulce ex citriis (pork stew with citron, grape must, leeks and spices) and the delicious oplontis, a ricotta, honey and candied fruit dessert reconstructed from a wall painting in the Roman town of the same name.

All the dishes have been culled from classical sources, like Apicius' De re coquinaria (The Art of Cooking). Attention is paid to detail, and so even the cutlery is Roman: no forks, but a lethal carving knife (a culter) and a spoon with a handle ending in a sharp point (cochlear) for spearing meat and winkling snails out of shells. Alas, however, guests do not recline on couches, and there are no naked concubines of either gender (well, at least not on our visit).

This place, while interesting, does have its weaknesses. The house wine – billed as 'Falernum' (a legendary Roman white) – is in fact an uninspiring Frascati; the wines on the list that includes only grape varieties known to the ancient Romans add a surcharge to an already well-leavened bill. In fact, The price per head – which includes all the food, water (unless you want it sparkling), house wine and service – goes down progressively the larger your party; a table of four will pay 45.50 each. At lunch and during the early dinner 'gustaticium' from 6 to 8pm, a lighter buffet-style meal is offered at the more reasonable price of 25- 29. Dinner should be booked ahead. For more on classical Roman cuisine, see p184 **Another dormouse, anyone?**

Magna Roma

Via Capo d'Africa 26 (06 700 9800/www.magnaroma.com). Metro Colosseo or bus/tram to via Labicana. **Meals served** *Oct-Mar 6-8pm, 8.30-11.30pm Tue-Sat; 12-2.30pm, 6-8pm, 8.30-11.30pm Sun. Apr-Sept 12-2.30pm, 6-8pm, 8.30-11.30pm daily.* **Average** . **Credit** *AmEx, DC, MC, V.*

Indian Restaurant

Typical Indian cuisine in an elegant atmosphere,
located not far from the Colosseum. Special Indian dishes
include chicken tikka masala, lamb vindaloo, chicken maharaja
tandoori and makhani paneer. Attentive and courteous service.
Open every day

❖ ❖ ❖

Via dei Serpenti, 124 • 00184 Roma
Tel: 06/47.47.144 Fax: 06/47.88.53.93
**In Venice: Maharani • Via G. Verdi,
97/99 • 30171 Mestre Venezia**
Tel: 041/98.46.81 Fax: 041/95.86.98
http://mall4all.com/maharajah

The best cakes

Bernasconi
See p104.

Mondi
See p196.

Vitti
See p48.

Dagnino
See p120.

Antonini
See p129.

wood, precarious perspex chairs and those all too familiar twigs set the design tone. The menu is split into four main sections: Mediterranean, Oriental, oceanic and sushi/sashimi. The idea is to mix and match, so linguine al pesto rosso con acciughe e pinoli (with red pesto and anchovies) might be followed by tasty Thai-style green curry prawns, or trancio di spada con avocado e salsa di lime (swordfish steak with avocado and lime sauce). A Pacific salad was spoiled by limp lettuce, but things look up at dessert time, with a succulent 'fruit tower' of wild berries in a sponge case. F.I.S.H. gives off a friendly vibe, and has an honest pricing policy. There are plans to open for lunch from September 2002.

Hosteria degli Artisti ★

Via G Sommeiller 6 (06 701 8148). Bus/tram to Porta Maggiore. **Meals served** 12.30-3.30pm, 7.30-11.30pm daily. Closed Sun in Aug. **Average** €€. **Credit** MC, V.
In a nondescript residential street not far from Porta Maggiore, this good-value southern Italian restaurant is quite simply a hidden treasure. It looks like the inside of a Neapolitan Christmas crib, but the food is more serious than the decor, putting the accent on the cuisine of northern Campania (south of Rome, north of Naples). Dishes here are unique, and worth seeking out. Take, for instance, the 'mpepata di cozze (peppery mussel soup), pasta e patate con provola affumicata (pasta and potato bake with smoked cheese) and the alici fritte (fried anchovies). The guy who runs the place has a gruff edge, but it's a surface thing: melt him by getting him going on to the subject of mozzarella di bufala, or, for that matter, on Campanian cuisine in general.

Monti, Termini & San Giovanni

Hosteria Ulderico

Via San Giovanni in Laterano 106 (06 7045 0935).
Metro Colosseo or bus/tram to via Labicana. **Meals
served** noon-3pm, 7.30-10.30pm Mon-Fri; noon-3pm Sat.
Closed Aug. **Average** €€. **No credit cards**.

Ulderico's is one of those local gems with a typical Roman
menu of traditional food where you will be won over by
the simpatia of the family. Mario Cicconi, his sister Paola
and their respective spouses cook and serve. Bucatini
all'amatriciana (pasta with a bacon and tomato sauce),
spaghetti alla carbonara (with egg, bacon and parmesan)
and spaghetti con le vongole (with clams) are among the
traditional, dependable primi; good secondi include
coniglio alla cacciatore (rabbit in wine and rosemary
sauce) and ossobuco con funghi (stewed calf's shanks
with mushrooms). There is always a good selection of
fresh vegetables as contorni: try the cicoria ripassata in
padella (greens sautéd with garlic and chili) or the carciofi
alla romana (artichokes with mint, parsley and garlic
stuffing) in late winter and early spring. The clientele
includes locals, Irish priests from the nearby college of
San Clemente, and intrepid tourists.

Il Quadrifoglio

*Via del Boschetto 19 (06 482 6096). Metro Cavour/bus to
Via Nazionale.* **Meals served** 7-11pm Mon-Sat. Closed
Aug. **Average** €€€. **Credit** AmEx, DC, MC, V.

If you can't make it to Naples, then this is the next best
thing. Il Quadrifoglio is one of the few places in Rome to
serve famed Neapolitan starters such as sartù (a baked
rice dish with a filling of egg, peas and tiny meatballs),
amply matched by main courses like involtini di cernia
al finochio selvatico (vegetable filled rolls of grouper
fillet flavoured with wild fennel). Typically southern
cuisine also characterises the vegetarian section of the
menu: try melanzane agrodolci alle mandorle (bitter-
sweet aubergine cooked with almonds). Desserts (served
with a complimentary glass of Muscat) are also a must,
though it's hard to choose between the sinful dolce
caprese (Caprese chocolate cake), the lighter dolce al
limone (a delicate lemon cake served with a light custard)
or the legendary babà (sponge cake soaked in rum). The
mark-up on wine is more than reasonable; all in all, Il
Quadrifoglio (the four-leaf clover) is indeed a lucky find.

La Piazzetta

*Vicolo del Buon Consiglio 23A (06 699 1640). Metro
Cavour/bus to via Cavour.* **Meals served** noon-3pm,
7-11pm Mon-Sat. Closed 2wks Aug. **Average** €€.
Credit MC, V.

A former well-known waiter at an ultra-traditional
restaurant for several years, Franco Bartolini decided to
strike out on his own a couple of years ago. The result is

Just around
the corner
from the wine
bar of the
same name
(*see p188*),
Trimani (via
Goito 20) is
Rome's best-
stocked wine
shop, though
prices are
rather high.

this small, elegant restaurant with soft lighting and a warm, cosy atmosphere, in a medieval lane between the Colosseum and via Cavour. In summer, the tables outside book up days in advance, but book whenever you come as this place is always popular – it's packed even on rainy winter Mondays. On entering, you'll be confronted with a large antipasto buffet; after securing a table, grab a plate and help yourself. The pasta comes in generous portions: the vermicelli alla tarantina, with mussels, clams, cherry tomatoes and fresh basil. Secondi include perfectly cooked fish like oven-baked turbot (rombo) with potatoes. But make sure you leave space for dessert: Sicilian pastry-chef Enrico Lalicata does an excellent selection of own-made cakes and biscuits, plus what is probably the best crème brûlée in town.

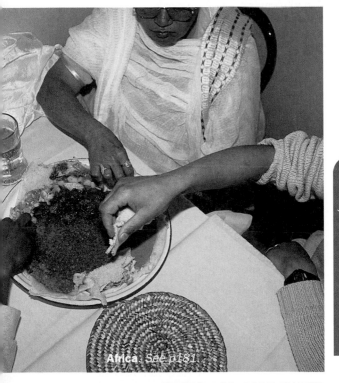

Africa. See p181.

Taverna Sottovento

Via Ciancaleoni 31 (06 474 2265). Metro Cavour/ bus to via Milano. **Meals served** 12.30-2.30pm, 7-11.30pm Mon-Sat. Closed 1wk Aug. **Average** €€. **Credit** AmEx, DC, MC, V.

This Calabrian restaurant in one of those narrow Monti lanes between Santa Maria Maggiore and Trajan's Market has a nautical-themed, wood-panelled dining room in a sunken space that seems to be an old courtyard. The excellent cuisine here is full of southern flavour, and gets you away from those standard Roman dishes that can tend to cloy after a short period of time. Most dishes are based on specially delivered Calabrian products, some of which are available for sale upstairs. Among the primi, the tagliolini with courgette flowers and scampi stand out; main courses are mainly fish-based: the rombo in crosta di patate (turbot in a roast potato case) is especially good. Vegetarians will also find a variety of options.

After hours

Late is a relative concept. Italians eat late by British or German standards but not nearly as late as the Spanish. In fact, after 11pm you'll be hard pressed to find an open restaurant outside of the divey tourist traps around the Spanish Steps. There is a strict code as to when people eat here, and you'd best figure it out if you don't want to starve. Families – even those with kids – eat dinner between 8pm and 10pm, and restaurant opening hours staunchly reflect this.

As with every rule, though, there are exceptions to this one, but if you want to eat your dinner much after 11pm, you have to know where to go. We're happy to help. We've compiled a handful of generally trustworthy places that can almost always be counted on to serve you until 1am or later.

Al Forno della Soffitta 1.30am (*see p199*).
Alle Fratte di Trastevere 1.30am; from May to mid-Sept only (*see p134*).
Baires 1am (*see p70*).
Borgo Antico 1am; Thur-Sat only (*see p123*).
Bruschetteria degli Angeli 1am (*see p84*).
Da Francesco 1am (*see p69*).
Da Ivo 1am (*see p142*).
Del Frate 1am (*see p128*).
Gusto 1am (*see p36*).
Il Bicchiere di Mastai 1am (*see p73*).
Il Brillo Parlante 1am (*see p43*).
Il Cantuccio 2am (*see p59*).
Il Leonardo 1am (*see p199*).
Panattoni 2am (*see p145*).
Pizza Ciro 1.30am (*see p33*).
Riparte Café 2am (*see p142*).
Sciam 1am (*see p98*).

Trattoria Monti ★

Via di San Vito 13A (06 446 6573). Metro Vittorio/bus to Santa Maria Maggiore. **Meals served** 12.45-2.45pm, 7.45-10.45pm Tue-Sat; 12.45-2.45pm Sun. Closed Aug. **Average** €€. **Credit** AmEx, DC, MC, V.

Just around the corner from the bustle of piazza Vittorio, Trattoria Monti is a quiet culinary haven. The menu centres on classics from Le Marche, with some imaginative surprises. The meat sauce in the tagliatelle con ragù marchigiano is extremely good, while the tagliolini con alici, pecorino di fossa e sultanine (egg pasta with fresh anchovies, seasoned pecorino cheese and sultanas) will satisfy the more adventurous palate. Main courses include such winter-warmers as stinco di bue al vino rosso (ox shank cooked in red wine), though the petto di tacchino all'aceto balsamico e lattughella (turkey breast cooked in a balsamic vinegar and lettuce sauce) makes for a (slightly) lighter option. Mark-ups on wine are fair, and the house Verdicchio is perfectly drinkable. Friendly service and the favourable quality/price ratio make this neighbourhood trat justifiably popular with locals and with tourists in the know. Booking is advised.

International

Africa

Via Gaeta 26-8 (06 494 1077). Metro Castro Pretorio/ bus to piazza dell'Indipendenza. **Meals served** noon-4pm, 7-11.30pm Tue-Sun. Closed 2wks Aug. **Average** €. **Credit** AmEx, MC, V.

Cheerfully casual, with sunset yellow tablecloths and silhouette murals of African fauna, this restaurant serves up simple Eritrean and Ethiopian cuisine. After falafel, served with a spicy dip, you can tuck into spongy, whole-wheat taita bread: the idea is to break pieces off and use them to scoop up the meat or vegetables, but someone will give you a fork if you need one. Try the mixed vegetarian plate, which comes with delicious stewed lentils. The Tibsi – grilled veal with spicy sauce – is also good. Sweet sesame halva, served with a cup of spicy tea, makes a good end to the meal.

Charly's Saucière

Via San Giovanni in Laterano 268-70 (06 7049 5666). Metro San Giovanni/bus to piazza San Giovanni. **Meals served** 7.45-11pm Mon, Sat; 12.45-2.15pm, 7.45-11pm Tue-Fri. Closed 2wks Aug. **Average** €€€. **Credit** AmEx, DC, MC.

One of Rome's few French restaurants, Charly's is best seen as a culinary refuge for those who have had enough of the trattoria. Its traditional, well-executed menu and simple but classy atmosphere are a bit of an anomaly on this heavily trafficked street near the Basilica of San Giovanni. White-haired chef Charly emerges from the kitchen periodically to bonsoir his guests and to prepare the excellent tartare main course and flambé desserts at your table. A light cheese soufflé, an onion soup with melted cheese or a pâté all make good, if substantial, starters. The main course menu is heavy on beef, which comes exclusively from Tuscan Chianina cattle: try the fillet with herb sauce or morels. The chef's Swiss origins show up in the fondues and the rösti potatoes. An evenly divided French-Italian wine cellar holds some 400 labels, ranging from a Château d'Yquem '83 (around €1,000) to the house Beaujolais (€13).

Guru

Via Cimarra 4-6 (06 474 4110). Metro Cavour/bus to via Nazionale. **Meals served** 7pm-midnight daily. **Average** €€. **Credit** AmEx, DC, MC, V.
If you're dying for an Indian, Il Guru will fill the gap... though probably no better than your local curry house back home. The cuisine is standard pan-Indian, done at a decidedly standard level of competence. But there's a proper tandoori oven, the staff are friendly, and it's cheap even by Roman standards. There are three fixed menus: vegetarian (€16), meat (€18) and fish (€20). But as the menu says, 'no sharing please'. You have been warned.

Hasekura ★

Via dei Serpenti 27 (06 483 648). Metro Cavour/bus to via Nazionale. **Meals served** noon-2.30pm, 7-10.30pm Mon-Sat. Closed Aug. **Average** €€. **Credit** AmEx, DC, MC, V.
The decor might not be old Kyoto, but the food at Hasekura is about the most authentically Japanese that you will find in the city. Partners Ito Kimiji (kitchen) and Franca Palma (up front) serve beautifully presented dishes to tourists and curious Italians alike. Good bets are the fixed-price set menus (tempura dinner €31, soba dinner €33.50; lunchtime menus are cheaper). The soba and tempura options are excellent, though for fish lovers the sushi and sashimi – prepared before your eyes – are hard to resist. Cold Asahi beer and/or warm sake provide suitable accompaniment. Specialities can be ordered if you phone ahead.

Indian Fast Food

Via Mamiani 11 (06 446 0792). Metro Vittorio/bus or tram to piazza Vittorio. **Meals served** 11am-4pm, 5-10pm Mon-Sat. **Average** €. **No credit cards**.
This is Rome's only Indian takeaway (at least it's the only one we could find), just off piazza Vittorio. You can eat in too, if you choose. The menu is basic Indian cuisine –

HAR
LAGER

GORDON'S
LONDON
DRY GIN

The Fiddler's Elbow. *See p188.*

Monti, Termini & San Giovanni

dahl, lamb curries and so on – accompanied by gloriously kitsch Indian music videos. You can even send a moneygram to Mumbai while you wait for your samosas.

Maharajah

Via dei Serpenti 124 (06 4747 144). Metro Cavour/ bus to via Nazionale. **Meals served** 12.30-2.30pm, 7-11.30pm Mon-Fri; 7-11.30pm Sat, Sun. **Average** €€. **Credit** AmEx, DC, MC, V.

Next door to the Guru (*see p182*), this other Monti Indian has the culinary edge, but is also a tad more expensive. The Maharajah scores points both for the welcoming service and the bright ethnic decor. The classic Punjabi menu includes good lamb rogan josh and a range of tandoori oven specialities. There are two fixed menus: meat-based (€30) and vegetarian (€28).

Pizzerie

Est! Est!! Est!!!

Via Genova 32 (06 488 1107). Metro Repubblica/bus to via Nazionale. **Meals served** 7pm-midnight Tue-Sun. Closed 3wks Aug. **Average** €€. **Credit** MC, V.

Usefully placed between the station and piazza Venezia, Est! Est!! Est!!! (named after the much-hyped but decidedly underwhelming wine of the same name) was renovated a few years back, but with the same dark wood fittings and the same starched, elderly waiters, it hasn't

Another dormouse, anyone?

'The dishes for the first course included an ass of Corinthian bronze with two panniers, green olives on one side and black on the other… There were some small iron frames shaped like bridges supporting dormice sprinkled with honey and poppy seed. There were steaming hot sausages too, on a silver gridiron with damsons and pomegranate seeds underneath.'

Trimalchus' lavish banquet in Petronius' racy sex 'n' food romp *The Satyricon* has long set the agenda for the popular, Hollywood-fuelled conception of

Roman eating habits. But Gaius Petronius' intent was to puncture the nouveau-riche pretensions of his puerile host, and the menu Trimalchus' slaves serve up can hardly be taken as representative.

In fact, apart from a predilection for spices and the absence of that post-Columbian import, the tomato, the diet of the ancient Romans was not that different from the diet of modern Italy. Emmer, spelt and barley (the first two are unrefined ancestors of today's transgenic wheat) were its staples, baked into bread

For excellent takeaway pizza, head for Nadia e Davide (via Milano 33), just off via Nazionale. Alongside the usual toppings are some gourmet options, including funghi porcini and salmon.

lost its old, slightly dour feeling that gives you the sense that this is a place where commercial travellers from out of town have been stopping to eat since the 1930s. The pizzas and calzoni ripieni (folded-over pizzas) are still good here, but, exclamation points aside, there is still a pervasive air of tiredness here.

La Gallina Bianca

Via Antonio Rosmini 9 (06 474 3777). Metro Termini/bus to Santa Maria Maggiore. **Meals served** noon-3pm, 6.30pm-midnight daily. **Average** €. **Credit** AmEx, DC, MC, V.

With its cute farm-theme decorations, waitresses in blue and white gingham aprons and – by Roman standards anyway – its vast dining room, this pizzeria-griglieria would slot comfortably into any American shopping mall. But if you've just stepped off the train at nearby Termini station, or you have built up an appetite looking around Santa Maria Maggiore, this pizza place will fill that gap in reliable, no-nonsense style. The thicker than average pizza, which comes in 20 varieties, is OK – although it's not knock-you-down-brilliant. Alternatively, you could always order a plain focaccia and supplement it with vegetable antipasti from the ample buffet. There are steaks, some standard pasta dishes and regular pizzeria extras like bruschette or suppli. The simple menu, efficient service and bearable-if-high noise level make it a good place to bring kids.

or mixed with water to form unleavened, pasta-like sheets. Fresh vegetables, fruit and olive oil were just as important as they are today, though the ever-present garum – a pungent sauce made from the fermented juices of salted mackerels or anchovies — has disappeared; its nearest cousins today are Far Eastern fish sauces like the Vietnamese nuoc mam.

Wine was an important part of the Roman meal, and of classical Italy's agricultural economy. The most highly prized wine-growing area was Massico, north of Naples, which produced the legendary Falernum. Most Roman wine was white, and almost all of it was sweet – a process encouraged by long ageing (up to a century, for the most robust vintages) and the storing of amphorae in lofts above the fireplace, where the heat would provoke a kind of rapid oxidisation or 'madeirisation'.

Finally, the wine was often mixed with spices, wood resin (as in the Greek retsina), herbs or honey – generally to disguise its inferior quality.

Monti, Termini & San Giovanni

Antico Caffè del Brasile. *See p189.*

Wine bars & pubs

Al Vino al Vino
Via dei Serpenti 19 (06 485 803). Metro Cavour/bus via Nazionale. **Open** 11am-2.30pm, 5pm-1.30am daily. Closed 3wks Aug. **Credit** MC, V.
This wine bar on lively via dei Serpenti has a range of more than 500 wines, with 25 available daily by the glass. But its real speciality are distillati, with dozens of fine grappas, whiskies and other spirits. In the dining room are pretty cast-iron tables topped with lava and ceramic. The menu here is strong on Sicilian specialities such as caponata (a sort of Sicilian ratatouille) and parmigiana (aubergines with parmesan gratin).

Cavour 313 ★
Via Cavour 313 (06 678 5496). Metro Cavour/bus to via Cavour. **Open** *Oct-May* 12.30-2.30pm, 7.30pm-12.30am Mon-Sat; 7.30pm-12.30am Sun. *June, July, Sept* 12.30-2.30pm, 7.30pm-12.30am Mon-Sat. Closed Aug. **Credit** AmEx, DC, MC, V.

A friendly atmosphere (despite the gloomy mahogany all about), a serious cellar and good snacks explain the eternal popularity of this wine bar at the Forum end of via Cavour. Prices are reasonable, and there's a big selection of hot and cold snacks; in winter, this place is especially strong on soups. With over 500 bottles on the wine list, which to choose is the only problem.

Divinare

Via Ostilia 4 (06 709 6281). Metro Colosseo or bus/tram to via Labicana. **Open** 10.30am-3.30pm, 5-9pm Mon-Thur; 10.30am-3.30pm, 5-11.30pm Fri, Sat. Closed 2wks Aug. **Credit** AmEx, DC, MC, V.

The small residential enclave just to the west of the Colosseum is slowly changing from working class to urban professional. Divinare is a good indication of the mutation. For years this was the local watering hole, with rough Castelli wine from the barrel and a few tables where old men played scopa over a simple plate of pasta. Now it is a sophisticated wine bar and restaurant, with a good choice of wines by the glass and interesting dishes for a light lunch or dinner. In a minuscule kitchen, chef Angelo Cavaterra and his wife prepare cheese platters, taster selections of cured meats and wild game carpaccio, and unusual salads. This is also a good place for vegetarians, with a selection of items like cheese and vegetable crêpes. Bottles are stacked up to the ceiling: more than 700 different crus are available to drink in or take away, plus small farm-made olive oils, handmade pasta and organic jams. You can generally count on spending around €18 for a light meal.

The Druid's Den

Via San Martino ai Monti 28 (06 4890 4781). Bus to piazza Santa Maria Maggiore. **Open** 5pm-2am daily.
No credit cards.

Like its cousin below (both are now under the same ownership), this is a pub that was already well established before the current craze for all things Irish. A decent pint of Liffey water, plus live football from both the Italian and British leagues.

The Fiddler's Elbow

Via dell'Olmata 43 (06 487 2110). Bus to piazza Santa Maria Maggiore. **Open** 5pm-1am daily.
No credit cards.

The first Irish pub in Italy, and still one of the most authentic. Italian students and homesick expats crowd on to benches in the smoky, narrow, wooden interior. There's a pool table in the back, a screen for TV sports events, and live music: Irish on Wednesday evenings and jazz on Sunday afternoons.

Shamrock

Via Capo d'Africa 26D (06 700 2583). Metro Colosseo or bus/tram to via Labicana. **Open** 7pm-2am daily.
No credit cards.

Shamrock is an old trouper on the Roman pub scene. Happy hour runs from 7pm to 9pm, but the place really starts to fill up around 10pm with noisy young Italians, plus the occasional Irish priest and – on Thursday evenings – sailing enthusiasts. Guinness on tap and a good selection of bottled beers can be soaked up with a hamburger, french fries or Irish stew. Darts (freccette) are taken seriously here; trophies abound, and owner Gianfranco Guarnaccia says his pub is the most important darts club in central and southern Italy. There is occasional live music and, happily enough, there are tables outdoors in the summer.

Trimani Wine Bar

Via Cernaia 37B (06 446 9630). Bus to via Cernaia/ via Goito. **Open** *Jan-Nov* 11.30am-12.30am Mon-Sat. *Dec* 11.30am-12.30am daily. Closed 2wks Aug.
Credit AmEx, DC, MC, V.

Pacific Trading Co (viale Principe Amedeo 17-21) is one of the biggest and best of the oriental supermarkets that surround piazza Vittorio.

This wine bar offshoot of Rome's leading enoteca (wine shop) is looking a bit shabby, especially upstairs, and service can be infuriatingly slow. But it still offers an excellent choice of Italian regional wines at reasonable (though not enoteca) prices, and a range of decent pasta dishes, quiches, soups and crostini. Tends to work better at lunch than dinner, though the new non-stop opening times allow for all-day snacking and imbibing.

Bars & cafés

Antico Caffè del Brasile ★
Via dei Serpenti 23 (06 488 2319). Metro Cavour/bus to via Nazionale. **Open** *Sept-June* 6am-8.30pm Mon-Sat; 7am-2pm Sun. *July, Aug* 6am-8.30pm Mon-Sat. Closed 2wks Aug. **No credit cards.**
Despite EU rules that ban the use of its centrepiece – a massive, wooden coffee-toasting machine – this torrefazione (coffee roastery) on the characterful main street of Monti still retains the same traditional atmosphere as it has since the early 20th century. Among its former clientele was the current Pope, while he was still humble Cardinal Wojtyla.

Bar/buffet del Palazzo delle Esposizioni
Via Milano 9 (06 482 8001/8207). Bus to via Nazionale. **Open** *Bar* 10am-9pm Mon, Wed-Sun. *Buffet* 12.30-3pm Mon, Wed-Sun. **Credit** AmEx, DC, MC, V.

The best — aperitivo bar

Rosati
See p48.

Le Grand Bar del St Regis Grand
See p120.

Ciampini al Café du Jardin
See p47.

Ombre Rosse
See p154.

La Vineria
See p101.

Monti, Termini & San Giovanni

The excellent bar at this major arts centre is a hotspot for local office staff, who also squeeze into the glass lift to eat at the smart, bright buffet restaurant upstairs. The entrance for those who are not also visiting exhibitions is on the left of the palazzo, halfway up the stairs that flank the road tunnel. The bar has fresh rolls, cakes and a decent selection of wines. Upstairs, the usual selection of salads, ready-to-eat pasta dishes and secondi are served up in an artsy canteen ambience. The food wouldn't win any prizes, but it's reasonably priced: expect to pay €12 for a light lunch.

Café Café

Via dei Santi Quattro 44 (06 700 8743). Metro Colosseo/bus or tram to piazza del Colosseo. **Open** 10am-1.30am Tue-Sun. Closed Aug. **Credit** MC, V.
A pleasant change from the usual chrome and glass counters, this attractive locale offers teas, wines, salads and sandwiches for travellers weary after a romp around the Colosseum. There's a brunch buffet on Sundays.

Café Renault

Via Nazionale 183B (06 4782 4452). Bus to via Nazionale. **Open** 8am-11.30pm Mon-Thur; 8am-1am Fri, Sat. Closed 2wks Aug. **Credit** AmEx, DC, MC, V.
Architecture buffs have long admired this early 20th-century glass and iron structure, which in a previous incarnation was a car showroom (hence the tag). Now reopened after a thorough makeover, this slick venue offers different seating areas for those who want to linger over a latte, grab an aperitivo (the range of cocktails is impressive) or take advantage of the lunchtime €7 help-yourself buffet of salads, veggie dishes and bakes. With music events and sundry other special evenings planned, Café Renault marks a further stage in the relaunch of the via Nazionale district – until recently a daytime-only shopping and office ghetto.

Caffetteria Nazionale

Via Nazionale 26-7 (06 4899 1716). Metro Repubblica/bus to via Nazionale. **Open** 8am-9pm Mon-Sat. **Meals served** 12.30-3pm. Closed 2wks Aug. **Credit** AmEx, DC, MC, V.
On one of the city's busiest thoroughfares, the Caffetteria Nazionale offers the usual bar fare during the day. But most punters arrive at lunchtime and head straight for the exceptionally well-laden buffet table, where a mixed plate of salad, vegetables au gratin, omelettes and cheeses can be piled up for €7.50-€10. As this is also the dining room of the adjacent Artemide Hotel, the anodyne international decor might not be as quaintly Roman as elsewhere, but the air-conditioned, efficient atmosphere is a relief from the shopping and tourist treadmill.

Suburbs

North

(Trionfale, Monte Mario,
Flaminio, Parioli, Salario)

Al Ceppo

*Via Panama 2 (06 841 9696). Bus/tram to piazza
Ungheria.* **Meals served** 12.45-3pm, 7.45-11pm
Tue-Sun. Closed 3wks Aug. **Average** €€€.
Credit AmEx, DC, MC, V.

This elegant restaurant run by the Milozzi sisters is the
culinary hub of Parioli, Rome's fur coat and Barbour
ghetto. It's a class act, though tourists tend to be treated
with less grace than return customers. The food should
not disappoint: the reworking of cucina marchigiana –
cuisine from the Marches, with much use of mushrooms,
fresh vegetables and seafood – is bold and original.
Dishes change seasonally; in spring, try the fettucine with
broad beans, ham and pecorino. Secondi are dominated
by dishes of fish and game.

Baja

*Lungotevere Arnaldo da Brescia (06 3260 0118).
Metro Flaminio/bus to Ponte Margherita.* **Meals
served** 8pm-midnight Tue-Sat. *Bar* 10pm-2am Tue-Sat.
Average €€€. **Credit** AmEx, DC, MC, V.

In the Dolce Vita years, converted Tiber barges were the
place to eat, drink and party. River pollution and the rise
of the seaside sent these floating nightclubs into forced
retirement; but recently Romans have begun to
rediscover their river, and Baja is one of the results.
Access is from a badly lit flight of steps at the Ponte
Margherita end of the Tiber-side road. Tables spill out
on to the deck in summer. The menu has Latin American
touches, with a large selection of Argentinian beef dishes.
Seafood dominates though, as in the salmon carpaccio
marinated in pink grapefruit. The tortino di spigola con
ortaggi (crustless pie of sea bass with vegetables) is a
fresh alternative to a basic fish fillet. And the chocolate
cake with 'caramelized' bananas (here meaning sliced
bananas with caramel sauce drizzled on top) offers a
super-sweet, indulgent wrap.

Brick-a-bar

*Via Basento 56 (06 8530 3349). Bus to via Po/tram
to viale Regina Margherita.* **Meals served** 12.30-3pm,
7.30pm-midnight Mon-Sat. Closed Aug. **Average** €€€.
Credit AmEx, DC, MC, V.

This new Arab-Mediterranean restaurant offers high-
level cuisine in a sleek ethnic setting, far from the

Baja

madding crowd. One of the house specialities is the title
dish, brick – otherwise known as briq à l'oeuf – a
delicious Tunisian appetiser that consists of an egg fried
with other ingredients (such as spinach) inside a filo
pastry parcel. Another is keftha, sardine dumplings in
tomato sauce. But there are also some more familiar
Sicilian pasta dishes, including risotto with roast
calamari, or pasta with prawns, wild fennel and cumin.
Save room for the fresh sorbets and hot apple torte.

Duke's

*Viale Parioli 200 (06 8066 2455). Bus to viale
Parioli/tram to piazza Ungheria.* **Meals served** 8pm-
midnight Mon-Fri, Sun. Closed 1wk Aug. **Average** €€.
Credit AmEx, MC, V.
On a main street in posh Parioli, Duke's claims to serve
'cucina Californiana'. But this trendy bar/restaurant is
clearly the brainchild of an Italian. The California rolls
offer yet another creative variation on this deeply
misunderstood dish – this version has tuna, cucumber and
carrot – and the caesar salad comes with chicken and the
strange addition of mint. Still, the place is modern and
breezy, and on a warm summer night the courtyard out

the back could almost be mistaken for a West Coast beach joint. The whir of blenders whipping up frozen concoctions and the beautiful, overtanned clientele five-deep at the bar add to the illusion. In a nod to the theme, the menu includes a selection of Californian wines.

Fauro

Via R Fauro 44 (06 808 3301). Bus to viale Parioli/ tram to piazza Ungheria. **Meals served** 12.30-3pm, 8-11.30pm Mon-Sat. Closed 2wks Aug. **Average** €€€. **No credit cards**.

In a narrow side street running parallel to chi-chi viale Parioli, Fauro is easy to miss. But don't be fooled by the out-of-the-way location, plain decor and overly familiar waiters: this is one of Rome's best seafood restaurants. The rombo sul passato di broccoli romaneschi e gelatina di pomodori (turbot on broccoli purée with tomato sauce) and orata al cartoccio (gilthead baked in tinfoil) are just two of the excellent main dishes. The wine list is designed with abbinamenti (food-wine matches) in mind. Service and preparation times are both slow – sometimes infuriatingly so – so expect to make a long evening of it, especially when the place is packed. In summer, a few tables squeeze on to the pavement. To secure one (indeed, to secure any table), book well ahead: and bring cash, as this place still has a 'no credit cards' policy.

Gaudì

Via Ruggiero Giovannelli 8-12 (06 884 5451). Bus to via Pinciana. **Meals served** 12.20-3pm, 7.30pm-midnight Mon-Fri; 7pm-midnight Sat, Sun. Closed for lunch in Aug. **Average** €-€€. **Credit** AmEx, DC, MC, V.

This bustling pizzeria on the edge of Villa Borghese has a casual, almost American feel that is fairly unusual for Rome. A popular spot among Romans for a relaxed meal out, its rooftop is converted into a huge terraced dining area during the warm season. A lightbulb hangs above each table and diners click it on, airplane-style, to signal to one of the student-aged waiting staff that they're ready to order. Select from 29 pizza choices, a whole slew of salads, and a wide selection of Neapolitan pasta dishes and grilled meats. Gaudì doesn't take reservations, so be prepared to queue if you get there after 8.30pm; lunchtimes are generally quieter.

Giallo Limone

Via Sabazio 22 (06 8424 2305). Bus to corso Trieste. **Meals served** 8-11.30pm Mon-Fri; 12.30-3pm, 7.30-11.30pm Sat. Closed 2wks Aug, 2wks Jan. **Average** €€. **Credit** AmEx, MC, V.

Walking into Giallo Limone (Lemon Yellow) is like stepping into a Van Gogh canvas. Bright yellow walls and blue wooden chairs create a sunny, slightly off-kilter

Bulzoni (viale Parioli 36) is considered by many to be the best enoteca (wine shop) in Rome. They also offer regular tastings and courses.

feel in this welcoming family-run bistro, nestled on a side street of the upscale Trieste neighbourhood. The food consists of traditional Mediterranean fare with a creative twist – as in the orecchiette con polpettine vegetali (ear-shaped pasta with vegetable balls). The €20 menu degustazione (dinner only) is a good deal; it comes with a number of creative antipasti (the mini-cheese soufflés dripping in honey are especially tasty), abundant half portions of pasta dishes and desserts. The bread – with walnuts or sultanas – is all freshly made. The menu changes daily – and thus is recited a voce (out loud).

Itoyo

Viale Regina Margherita 164 (06 854 1318). Bus to via Po/tram to viale Regina Margherita. **Meals served** noon-3pm, 7-11pm daily. **Average** €-€€. **Credit** AmEx, DC, MC, V.

Handy for the tram, this brand new Japanese restaurant has quality sushi on the cheap in a kid-friendly atmosphere. The Zen suggestions of the rice paper walls and ceiling are let down a little by the pine tables and benches; more authentic is the small, sunken private chamber, complete with slippers, which can be booked for parties of up to eight. As for the food, avoid the pasti completi such as the sashimi teshoku (€15) which comes with all courses on one tray, and stick with the teppan

Il Cigno. See p196.

yaki, which involves a table-top barbecue of meat, fish and vegetables. Or try the fresh sushi. If you are into salmon roe and sea urchins, go for the sushi matsu.

Il Cigno

Viale Parioli 16 (06 808 2348). Bus to viale Parioli. **Meals served** 7.30am-9pm daily. **Average** €. **Credit** AmEx, DC, MC, V.

Held in deep affection by the Fendi-wielding denizens of Parioli, the posh bar Il Cigno (The Swan) has – among its other notable qualities – a staggering 25 types of breakfast cornetto. If these don't strike your fancy, you can always opt for a lemon or coffee mousse or something a bit more savoury from the bar. Not just any bar – it's a marvellously elaborate affair with brass swans below and a marine scene in garishly coloured ceramic.

L'Ortica ★

Via Flaminia Vecchia 573L (06 333 8709). Bus to corso Francia. **Meals served** 8-11pm Mon-Sat. Closed 2wks Aug. **Average** €€€. **Credit** AmEx, DC, MC, V.

If there were a prize for the oddest Roman gourmet restaurant location, L'Ortica would win it hands down. To get there, head north across Mussolini's monumental Ponte Flaminio into busy corso Francia, and locate the Standa supermarket on your right. On the terrace above it – next door to a billiard parlour – stands Vittorio Virno's oasis of culinary excellence. The accent is Neapolitan – militantly so, with all the ingredients brought in fresh from trusted suppliers; they are put to excellent use in dishes such as squid stuffed with endive, sultanas and pine-nuts. Outside, a verdant terrace is screened from the surrounding suburban chaos.

Mondi ★

Via Flaminia 468A (06 333 6466). Bus or tram to via Flaminia. **Meals served** Oct-Mar 7am-10pm Tue-Sun. *Apr-Sept* 7am-midnight Tue-Sun. **Average** €. **Credit** AmEx, DC, MC, V.

Residents of the Cassia-Flaminia area swear this is the best bar-pasticceria in town. Specialities here include pasticceria mignon (mini-cakes) and croccanti mondini (croquant chocolate balls). The cakes and luscious semifreddi (frozen desserts) are true works of art.

Osteria del Rione

Via Basento 20 (06 855 1057). Bus to via Po. **Meals served** 12.30-2.30pm, 7-11.30pm Mon-Fri; 7-11.30pm Sat. Closed Aug. **Average** €. **No credit cards**.

The Osteria del Rione ('neighbourhood hostelry') is ideal for those sick of nouvelle cuisine who want to eat like a horse and drink like a fish for €15.50 per head (the price of the menu fisso), all within striking distance of the

The Roman branch of a celebrated Neapolitan cioccolatiere, **Gay-Odin** (via A Stoppani 9) has a range of tempting specialities, from chocolate oysters to a chocolate-rum Vesuvius.

Get posh at Beck's

'Vado a mangiare da Beck' (I'm going to eat at Beck's) has become the Roman gourmet's favourite phrase.

Beck, of course, is Heinz Beck, the German chef summoned in the mid 1990s to revitalise the rooftop restaurant at the Hilton Hotel, sitting like a luxury concrete bunker on the crest of Monte Mario. Within a few years, he had overturned the prejudices of local food critics and dragged La Pergola to the top of the restaurant league, where it now sits in solitary, uncontested splendour.

The plaudits are merited: Beck marries technical dexterity with an inspired understanding of taste and texture. His philosophy comes through in the panaché di pesce all'olio di basilico – an antipasto selection of fish served in a light pesto. The dish is accompanied by two amuse-gueules: one of cold puréd tomato with a twist of artichoke ice-cream, the other of diced tomato with artichoke mousse. In both, the play of taste and colour melds well.

Despite the fact that he is known as 'the chef who doesn't do pasta', on a recent visit three out of seven primi were pasta dishes – including a melt-in-the-mouth tortellini di ricotta e pecorino con fave (with ricotta and pecorino cheeses, and broad beans). Guests can choose drinks from a mineral list, a tea list and a wine list in two volumes.

Along with outstanding food and excellent service, there is also a grand view over the whole of Rome, framed by elegant wooden columns.

In the end, Beck's place is not over-priced. Of course, it may sound odd to claim that 260 for a meal for two with a bottle of wine represents good value, but there are at least half a dozen places in Rome that charge similar prices for meals that are in a far lower league.

The best way to approach La Pergola – having booked a week in advance and rung the day before to confirm – is to go for one of the menu degustazioni (five courses 110, seven courses 125). These are Beck's party pieces, prepared with focus and served with theatrical pizzazz.

La Pergola ★
Hilton Hotel, Via Cadlolo 101 (06 3509 2211). Bus to piazzale Medaglie d'Oro. **Meals served** 7.30-10.30pm Tue-Sat. Closed 3wks Jan, 2wks Aug. **Average** . **Credit** AmEx, DC, MC, V.

Suburbs

Oriental Food Kosher. *See p202.*

Galleria Borghese. Just don't examine the glasses too carefully, nor expect spacious surroundings. If your Italian is a little shaky, bearded owner Bruno will recite the day's bill of fare in charming English. It always includes an array of antipasti such as bruschette, grilled vegetables and 'strong cheese', plus three pasta dishes, followed by 'meat-a-balls' and other forms of beef. The fixed menu includes all the wine you can drink, and if you are not too hammered by the time the freshly made dessert arrives, Bruno will suggest rounding things off with a dizzying glass of grappa.

East

(Nomentana, Università, Tiburtino, Prenestino, Casilina)

Al Forno della Soffitta

Via dei Villini 1E (06 440 4642). Metro Policlinico/bus to Porta Pia. **Meals served** 7am-1.30am Mon-Sat. Closed 2wks Aug. **Average** €€. **Credit** AmEx, DC, MC, V.
The original branch of this hugely popular pizzeria lies just outside Porta Pia on via Nomentana, not far from the British Embassy. The reason for its success is simple: the Neapolitan pizzas made here are among the best, and the most authentic, in town. Watch the exhibitionist pizzaioli spin the dough circles in the air to get the required shape, and try the end result, served on wooden platters that look like giant table-tennis bats. Upstairs is a proper Neapolitan restaurant, and extras (delicious antipasti and desserts, delivered fresh each day from Naples) and wines can be ordered downstairs as well. But if you do stray beyond pizza – or eat a full meal upstairs – the bill will leap beyond €20 with cover charge and service. No bookings are taken, and the place fills up early.

Il Leonardo ★

Via Catania 29 (06 4423 3705). Metro Bologna/bus to piazzale delle Provincie. **Meals served** 1-3pm, 8pm-1am Tue-Sat; 8pm-1am Sun. Closed 2-3wks Aug. **Average** €€€€. **Credit** AmEx, DC, MC, V.
As the adage goes, you can't judge a book by its cover, and from the outside, Il Leonardo looks rather nondescript, lost amid high apartment blocks in this residential area to the north of the centre. Once inside, the frosted mirrors and seriously heavy elegance of the place make for a striking contrast. The service is impeccable, the excellent wine list patiently explained by a sommelier who speaks good English, the background music

It's worth the trek out to Monte Sacro to sample the gourmet takeaway pizza served up by Angelo Iezzi, prophet of soya-based dough, at **Angelo e Simonetta** (via Nomentana 581).

San Lorenzo – ghetto glam

First a railway workers' ghetto, then a cut-price student hangout, the working-class enclave of San Lorenzo, just east of the station, has been attracting a smarter, more artsy bohemian crowd for the last ten years or so. Galleries and craft shops have opened here, bringing in a young, hip crowd particularly in the former Cerere pasta factory, which is the closest Rome comes to the New York loft scene. Alongside the pubs and bars, a slew of bistros has arisen to stoke the flame, so that serious Roman foodies now head for San Lorenzo rather than passé Trastevere.

Arancia Blu

Via dei Latini 55-65 (06 445 4105). Bus to via Tiburtina. **Meals served** 8.30-11.45pm daily. **Average** . **No credit cards**.
The nouvelle approach of this upmarket vegetarian restaurant is seen in a salad of puntarelle (chicory stems) with walnut balsamic vinegar dressing and aged piave cheese shavings: an interesting twist on a classic Roman salad. There's also an onion stuffed with ricotta, pecorino, pine nuts and parsley with a carrot and Humebashi vinegar sauce. There's an extensive dessert list – including a chocolate tasting menu with accompanying rum. One drawback is the service; one waiter literally grimaced at every request we made.

Il Dito e la Luna

Via dei Sabelli 47-51 (06 494 0726). Bus to via Tiburtina. **Meals served** 8pm-midnight Mon-Sat. Closed 3wks Aug. **Average** . **No credit cards**.
It's refreshing to come across a restaurant that thinks and operates like a ristorante, with informal, friendly service and prices more along the lines of a trattoria. The bistro atmosphere is intimate but not overly romantic; food is of the sunny, full-flavoured Sicilian variety. The flan di cipolle di tropea con fonduta di parmigiano (onion flan with parmesan sauce) makes for an appetising start to the meal, while the seafood and vegetable couscous offers a welcome change from pasta.

Marcello ★

Via dei Campani 12 (06 446 3311). Bus to via Tiburtina/tram to viale dello Scalo di San Lorenzo. **Meals served** 7.30pm-midnight Mon-Fri. Closed Aug. **Average** - . **No credit cards**.
From the outside it looks like one of these unpretentious, spit-and-sawdust places that Romans refer to as un buco – a hole in the wall. There's no name, just a sign reading 'Cucina'. Inside, old wooden tables are occupied by hordes of students from the nearby university. The menu offers Roman offal specialities like tripe, sweetbreads and pajata (baby veal intestines), along with creative dishes such as

straccetti ai carciofi (strips of veal cooked with fresh artichoke). The same goes for pasta like the ravioloni filled with fresh cheese, ricotta and walnuts. A surprisingly extensive wine list, strong on big reds, confirms that this place is a lot more than a buco.

Tram Tram
Via dei Reti 44-46 (06 490 416). Bus to piazzale Verano/ tram to via dei Reti. **Meals served** 12.30-3pm, 7.30-11.30pm Tue-Sun. Closed 2wks Aug. **Average** . **Credit** AmEx, DC, MC, V.

Taking its name from its proximity to the tram tracks, this good-value nouvelle trattoria attracts a young crowd, who are not fazed by the waiters' rather hassled manner. The menu derives much of its inspiration from Puglia (the heel of Italy), and so it is especially strong on fish and vegetables, as in the tagliolini calamaretti e pesto (pasta strips with baby squid and pesto).

Uno e Bino ★
Via degli Equi 58 (06 446 0702). Bus to via Tiburtina/tram to viale dello Scalo di San Lorenzo. **Meals served** 8.30-11.30pm Tue-Sun. Closed 3wks Aug. **Average** . **Credit** DC, MC, V.

Behind an unassuming façade lies one of Rome's best-value gourmet dinners. Dishes feature audacious combinations, as in the animelle tostate al timo e fagioli cannellini (toasted innards with thyme and cannellini beans) or the succulent tagliata di tonno al sesamo con i capperi e sformato di cavolfiore (seared tuna in sesame seeds, with capers and cauliflower). Excellent pasta courses include the pizzocheri di grano saraceno con fontina, patate e spinaci (wide buckwheat tagliatelle with fontina cheese, potatoes and spinach).

Suburbs

(generally a singer) pleasant and discreet. But above all, the food is an art form. The owner worked for years at the Sans Souci (*see p111*), and brought the chef and many of the waiters with him. The antipasti includes a fresh insalata di mare, a seafood salad with citrus fruits. The speciality pasta, ravioloni Leonardo, consists of five large ravioli, three filled with fish, two with vegetables. The menu also includes fish chowder and a selection of risottos. While seafood is the forté here (try the succulent turbot with endives), there's also a wide array of beef dishes. But save space for the fresh soufflés and tarts.

Oriental Food Kosher

Via Livorno 12 (06 440 4840/www.kosherinrome.it).
Metro Bologna/bus to via Livorno. **Meals served**
12.30-3pm, 6.30-11pm Mon-Thur, Sun; 12.30-3pm Fri;
6.30-11pm Sat. Closed Jewish holidays. **Average €.**
Credit AmEx, MC, V.
Morocco, Libya and Tunisia meet in this lively locale near piazza Bologna. It provides something unique in Rome: traditional Middle Eastern food with a Sephardic Jewish

Al Ponte della Ranocchia

Suburbs

twist, served either to eat in or take away. Houmous, baba ganoush and falafel are accompanied by warm pitta bread and a touch of spicy harissa. Sample them all by ordering the misto di salse. Some more exciting nights also feature belly dancing and live music.

Semidivino

Via Alessandria 230 (06 4425 0795). Bus to via Nomentana/corso Trieste. **Meals served** 1-3.30pm, 6.30pm-midnight Mon-Fri; 6.30pm-midnight Sat. Closed 3wks Aug. **Average** €. **Credit** DC, MC, V.
Just off corso Trieste near via Nomentana, this small wine bar has the feel of a French bistro, run though it is by two chatty Iranian brothers with a vast knowledge of wines. Alongside the extensive wine list, they also offer a limited but interesting selection of food. These generally include a couple of soup and pasta options, secondi like roulé di quaglia (quail roulé), a range of cured meats, various cheeses and unusual salads. Fresh desserts include crema calda con mele (warm apple custard) and gelato alla cannella (cinnamon ice-cream).

South

(Tuscolana, Appia, Ardeatino, Ostiense, EUR, Magliana)

Addo' Masto

Via Bove 43 (06 574 6372). Metro Piramide/bus to via Ostiense. **Meals served** 12.30-3pm, 7.30-11.30pm Tue-Sun. Closed 2wks Aug. **Average** €.
Credit AmEx, DC, MC, V.
Forget about attitude and gourmet angst: Addo' Masto is all about quantity, with a huge dining area that is matched by the size of the pizzas. Although there is an assortment of bruschette and fried antipasti, most appetites are more than satisfied with one of Addo's high-risers. These come with all the classic toppings – don't be afraid to mix and match, and it's all best accompanied by draught Nastro Azzurro or the (fairly) palatable house white from Ischia. Lunchtimes are quieter with a standard pasta menu replacing the evening-only pizza.

Al Ponte della Ranocchia ★

Circovallazione Appia 29 (06 785 6712). Metro Ponte Lungo. **Meals served** 12.30-2.30pm, 8-11.30pm Mon-Sat. Closed 1wk Aug. **Average** €€.
Credit AmEx, DC, MC, V.
Don't be fooled by the simple trattoria decor, with the hatch through to the kitchen and the 1930s-style

Suburbs

travertine facing on the walls. 'At the Bridge of the Frog' uses Jewish and Levantine influences to put a welcome spin on the local tradition, with much emphasis on fresh ingredients and a well-priced wine list. House speciality is the Ruota del Faraone, a lightly fried wheel of fettuccine with meat stock, goose meat, sultanas and pinenuts. Among other primi, the pappardelle con crema di cipolle, porcini e reggiano (pasta with onion sauce, porcini mushrooms and parmesan) are excellent. Secondi include aliciotti con l'indivia (anchovies with endives), and vegetarians are well served here too. Finish off with a plate of walnut-filled cannoncini alla romana biscuits. This is a working-class area of town where tourists rarely tread, but it is easily reached by metro.

Bishoku Kobo

Via Ostiense 110B (06 574 4190). Metro Garbatella/bus to via Ostiense. **Meals served** 7.30-10.30pm Mon-Sat. Closed 1wk Aug. **Average** €€. **No credit cards.**
This relatively new Japanese restaurant on via Ostiense is well placed for visitors to the statues in the adjacent Centrale Montemartini. Though the food is classic Japanese, the ambience is that of a neighbourhood trattoria (except for a few details, such as a gloriously kitsch sushi clock). The sashimi, sushi and stuffed vegetables are all good, and the tempura is well worth the extra wait. Prices are relatively low, and it's always packed with locals, so book ahead.

Bishoku Kobo

Cecilia Metella

Via Appia Antica 125 (06 513 6743). Bus to via Appia Antica. **Meals served** noon-3pm, 7-10.30pm Tue-Sun. Closed 2wks Aug. **Average** €€-€€€. **Credit** AmEx, DC, MC, V.
Just across the street from the catacombs of San Sebastiano, this long-running Appia Antica restaurant is one of the few to combine an obvious tourist orientation with an equally obvious concern for quality. Perched on top of a low-rising hill, with a vine-covered terrace for outdoor dining, Cecilia Metella is ideal for a lazy lunch after a visit to the catacombs or the nearby Circus of Maxentius. Service is swift and professional; specialities include scrigno alla Cecilia (baked green noodles swimming in cheese) and pollo al Nerone (flambéed chicken). The polenta ai porcini (polenta with porcini mushrooms) is also extremely moreish.

L'Apepiera

Via Latina 295B (06 789 060). Bus to via Latina. **Meals served** 7.30pm-midnight Mon-Sat. Closed 3wks Aug, 1wk Jan. **Average** €€. **Credit** AmEx, DC, MC, V.
This cozy, candlelit trattoria in the deeper reaches of the Appio Latino quartiere has a surprisingly international

More branches of the excellent **Al Forno della Soffitta** (*see p199*) can be found at via Piave 62-64 and via Luciani 52.

Suburbs

menu, in which creative Italian cucina casalinga (home cooking) merges with Greek and Polish influences. Owner-chef Signora Valente recites the evening's bill of fare; non-Italian speakers can request a written menu but will be missing most of the daily specials. Start with the foccaccine meridionali (southern-style pastry stuffed with cheese and ham) and move on to the pieroghi dell'Apepiera (stuffed potato dumplings with a spicy twist) followed by Greek-style moussaka, or the classic tagliata agli odori (grilled meat with herbs). Top it all off with slice of tortino di cioccolato (flaky chocolate tart).

Osteria del Velodromo Vecchio

Via Genzano 139 (06 7886 793). Metro Colli Albani/bus to via Genzano. **Meals served** 12.30-3pm, 8-11pm Mon-Sat. Closed Aug. **Average** €€. **Credit** MC, V.

A really friendly, good-value osteria near the site of a former cycling stadium – hence the name. Inside is one small room with eight tables; in summer, a few more are arranged outside on a sheltered patio. The cooking is solidly Roman, but alongside old favourites like pasta e fagioli (pasta and bean soup) or rigatoni con la pajata (rigatoni with baby veal intestines), there are a few more creative dishes, like fettucine tonno e zucchine (with tuna and courgettes). One or two dishes – like aliciotti e indivia (anchovies and endives) – reflect the Jewish contribution to the local tradition. Desserts consist of fresh crostate (pastry tarts), or aniseed ciambelline biscuits with a glass of sweet wine. The wine list here may be small but it's also surprisingly adventurous.

Palombini

Piazzale Adenauer 12 (06 591 1700). Metro Magliana/bus to piazza G Marconi. **Meals served** 7am-midnight daily. Closed 2wks Aug. **Average** €. **Credit** AmEx, MC, V.
EUR was built by Mussolini as a Fascist model suburb, and here, in the shadow of the imposing Palazzo del Civiltà del Lavoro (also known as the square Colosseum) stands this marble pavilion, surrounded by sweeping gardens. Its huge patio area, covered by a steel and plastic tent, is a favourite meeting point for young Romans – the nearest Rome gets to Beverly Hills, and not a bad

Pizza – Roman, Neapolitan

As if to compensate for the sacrilege of what passes for pizza abroad, Italian pizzaioli have – at least until recently – been fundamentalist keepers of the flame. Within each region, the local tradition was sacrosanct. So Genoa had its focaccia, Rimini the piadina, Florence the schiacciata, Naples, Milan and Turin had the high-rise pizza napoletana,

while Romans favoured the flat pizza romana. But things have become more fluid recently.

Ten years ago there was only one Neapolitan pizzeria in central Rome; now there are at least a dozen. The main difference is not so much in the dough as in the rolling: Roman pizzaioli roll their pizza uniformly flat, while the Neapolitans leave them

Cecilia Metella.
See p204.

or nouvelle?

thicker, especially at the edges. (In Naples, they attack a pizza by first separating this puffy frame from the body of the pizza, then eating everything inside it, so that they're left at the end with a circle of puffy dough; only the very hungry then go on to devour this too.)

However, there is now a Third Way, pioneered by Roman pizzaiolo Angelo Iezzi in the late 1980s. Iezzi was in the business of takeaway pizza; and the problem with pizza rustica (as the Romans call the takeaway version) is that unlike the restaurant variety, it tends to sit around for a while, and is generally reheated before serving. The result is often a hard, indigestible slab. From his shop in the distant Roman suburb of Monte Sacro, Iezzi began experimenting with different types of impasto (dough) and other variables.

Finally, with the help of supplier Corrado Di Marco, he came up with a dough based on a mixture of flours – including soya – which is left to rise for as long as 48 hours at low temperatures before it is ready for the oven. The resulting pizza – with which Iezzi won the national pizza championships two years running – is thicker than your average Roman pizza, but not heavy like the Neapolitan version. It also stays fresh for much longer.

You can sample this 'nouvelle pizza' at Iezzi's original takeaway shop, **Angelo e Simonetta** (via Nomentana 581) or at **Dar Poeta** in Trastevere (*see p143*), a sit-down pizzeria run by disciples of il maestro. For aspiring evangelists, Angelo Iezzi runs a five-week beginners' course at the Scuola Italiana Pizzaioli (via di Scorticabove 149; 06 4120 0838; www.pizza.it/api).

Suburbs

imitation – slick and modern and packed with the prettiest people Rome has to offer. As a gelateria, pasticceria and snack supplier, it's also first-rate.

Tramonti e Muffati ★

Via Santa Maria Ausiliatrice 105 (06 780 1342).
Metro Furio Camillo/bus to via Appia Nuova.
Meals served 8.30pm-midnight Mon-Sat. *Wine bar/deli* 4.30-8.30pm Mon-Sat. Closed Aug. **Average** €€.
Credit AmEx, DC, MC, V.

This tiny wine bar and delicatessen just off the Appia Nuova has built up a solid reputation in the five years since it opened. Behind the small shopfront are just five tables for evening dining; only 20 people can be accommodated, so it is worth booking well ahead. The owner here hunts obsessively for the best wines, bakery goods and farm products, which are presented pretty much as they come; these might include a selection of sott'oli (vegetables preserved in olive oil, including sun-dried tomatoes and stuffed pimentos); or a saccotto (a filo pastry bundle filled with ricotta and candied fruit) from an esteemed Roman bakery. These ready-to-go delicacies (most of which can also be bought here to take away) are supplemented by a few hot dishes, such as testaroli della Lunigiana (spongy pasta squares) with pesto sauce and pinoli, or cheese fondue flavoured with truffle shavings. But wine is the real point of the exercise – to the extent that the items on the menu are organised not by courses, but by what wine they best suit. The well-priced list features a number of small regional producers so obscure that even the best-informed wine buff might not know.

Zampagna ★

Via Ostiense 179 (06 574 2306). Metro San Paolo/bus to via Ostiense. **Meals served** 12.30-2.30pm Mon-Sat. Closed Aug. **Average** €. **No credit cards.**

There are two reasons for making a pilgrimage to the nether reaches of the via Ostiense: one is to see St Paul's Basilica and the other is to lunch here. Run by Maria Zampagna and family, this is basic Roman cooking as it once was – filling dishes for the confirmed carnivore. Primi include spaghetti alla carbonara or tagliatelle alla gricia (with bacon and pecorino cheese), while most of the second courses – whether bollito alla picchiapò (boiled beef with onions), involtini (rolls of meat stuffed with carrot and celery) or the inevitable, ultra-classic trippa (tripe) – are served swimming in the thick house sugo (tomato sauce). The broccoli ubriachi (literally, 'drunken broccoli'), tossed in wine with a sprinkle of chilli, make for an excellent side dish. Service is brisk, and the clientele are busy local workers.

GLOSSARY

Pasti (meals)
prima colazione	breakfast
pranzo	lunch
cena	supper
uno spuntino	a snack.

Basi e condimenti (basics and seasonings)
aceto	vinegar
aglio	garlic
basilico	basil
latte	milk
limone	lemon
miele	honey
olio d'oliva	olive oil
pane	bread
pepe	pepper
prezzemolo	parsley
sale	salt
zucchero	sugar

Modi di cottura (cooking techniques)
al dente	cooked, but firm (pasta)
al forno	baked
al sangue	rare (steaks)
al vapore	steamed

Glossary

alla griglia/grigliato/	
alla piastra	grilled
bollito	boiled
cotto	cooked
crudo	raw
fritto	fried
in umido/stufato	stewed
brasato	braised

Antipasti (hors d'oeuvre)

alici marinati	marinated anchovies
antipasto di mare	seafood hors d'oeuvre
antipasto misto	mixed hors d'oeuvre
bresaola	dry-cured beef
bruschetta	toast with garlic and oil
fiori di zucca	fried courgette flowers
olive ascolane	olives coated in breadcrumbs and mincemeat
pizzelle	puffy, bite-sized 'ravioli' of pizza dough
prosciutto cotto/	
crudo	cooked ham/cured ham
supplì	breadcrumb-coated rice croquettes with cheese and/or mincemeat.

Pizza toppings

calzone	a doubled-over pizza
capricciosa	ham, egg, olives
funghi	mushrooms
marinara	plain tomato
margherita	tomato and mozzarella
napoli or napoletana	tomato, anchovy and mozzarella
quattro formaggi	four cheeses (in theory)
quattro stagioni	mozzarella, artichoke, egg, mushrooms

Pasta

bavette/tagliolini	flat
bucatini	round, hollow
cannelloni	tubes
conchiglie	shells
farfalle	butterflies
maccheroni/	
rigatoni/ziti	fat tubes
maltagliati	short flat pasta
orecchiette	literally 'little ears'
pappardelle	thin tubes
ravioli/agnolotti	parcels
strozzapreti/pici	round, irregular
tonnarelli	square
vermicelli/spaghetti	round

Sughi e ripieni
(pasta sauces and fillings)

ai funghi porcini	mushrooms
ai quattro formaggi	four cheese sauce
all'arrabbiata	tomato and chilli
alla lepre	hare sauce
alla sorrentina	tomato and mozzarella
alle vongole	clams
ai frutti di mare	seafood
ricotta e spinaci	cottage cheese and spinach
al pesto	basil sauce
al pomodoro fresco	with raw tomatoes
al ragù	'alla bolognese', with minced meat and tomatoes
al sugo	puréed tomatoes
all'amatriciana	with tomato, guanciale, onion and pecorino cheese
alla gricia	the same but without tomato
all'arrabbiata	with tomato and chilli
alla carbonara	with pancetta and egg
alla puttanesca	with olives, capers, garlic in hot oil
cacio e pepe	pecorino and pepper

Carne, cacciagione (meat, game)

abbacchio/agnello	lamb
anatra	duck
capra, capretto	goat, kid
capriolo	roe deer
cinghiale	wild boar
coniglio	rabbit
faraona	guinea-fowl
fagiano	pheasant
guanciale	salted pork cheek lard

Glossary

maiale, maialino	pork, piglet
manzo	beef
oca	goose
pancetta	similar to bacon
pollo	chicken
prosciutto	ham
Parma	ham
quaglia	quail
tacchino	turkey
vitello/vitellone	veal

Cucina romana
(Roman meat and offal specialities)

coda alla vaccinara	oxtail braised in broth
pajata	a section of baby veal stomach with the mother's milk still inside, cooked in lard, onion, celery and parsley, and usually served with rigatoni
fagioli con le cotiche	beans with pork scratchings
insalata di zampi	hoof jelly salad
animelle	the spongy white pancreas and thymus glands, fried
tripa	tripe
cervello	brain
lingua	tongue
guanciale	cured pig's cheek
nervetti	strips of cartilage.

Piatti di carne (meat dishes)

bollito con salsa verde	boiled meat with parsley
carpaccio/bresaola	thin sliced cured beef
ossobuco	beef shins with marrow
polpette	meatballs
porchetta	roast piglet
rognoni trifolati	stir-fried kidneys
salsicce	sausages
saltimbocca	veal strips and ham
spezzatino	casseroled meat
spiedini	anything on a spit
straccetti	stir-fried beef or veal

Pesce (fish and seafood)

alici, acciughe	anchovies
baccalà	salt cod
branzino, spigola	sea bass
cape sante	scallops
calamari	squid
cozze	mussels

Glossary

gamberi	prawns
merluzzo	cod
pesce spada	swordfish
salmone	salmon
sogliola	sole
tonno	tuna
vongole	clams

Verdura/il contorno (vegetables/side dishes)

asparagi	asparagus
broccoli siciliani	broccoli
broccolo	green cauliflower
carciofi	artichokes
carote	carrots
cavolfiore	cauliflower
cetriolo	cucumber
fagioli/haricot/	
borlotti	beans
fave	broad beans
funghi	mushrooms
insalata	salad
melanzane	aubergines
patate	potatoes
peperoncino	chilli
peperoni	peppers
pomodori	tomatoes
rughetta/rucola	rocket
spinaci	spinach
zucchine	courgettes

Glossary

Index

Ad Index

Please refer to the relevant
pages for addresses and
telephone numbers.

Bus routes

© Copyright ATAC S.p.A. By kind permission.

Rome by Area

NORTH

Museo Nazionale di Villa Giulia

Galleria Nazionale d'Arte moderna

Stazione Roma-Viterbo

Villa Borghese

Piazza del Popolo

VATICAN, PRATI & WEST (p122)

VIA FLAMINIA

VIALE ANGELICO

Castel Sant'Angelo

Piazza di Spagna

TRIDENTE (p32)

Città del Vaticano

TREVI & VENETO (p106)

Museo Nazionale Romano

Stazione Termini

NAVONA (p50)

Piazza Navona

Fontana di Trevi

VIA DEL CORSO

VIA NAZIONALE

CORSO VITT. EMANUELE II

FIORI & GHETTO (p80)

Campidoglio

Foro Romano

MONTI, TERMINI & SAN GIOVANNI (p168-9)

Isola Tiberina

Teatro di Marcello

Colosseo

TRASTEVERE & MONTEVERDE (p132)

VIALE TRASTEVERE

Circo Massimo

Tevere

AVENTINE & TESTACCIO (p156)

Terme di Caracalla

Stazione Roma-Ostia

Stazione Ostiense

Fiume

CIRC. GIANICOLENSE

VIA OSTIENSE

SOUTH

CIRCONVALLAZIONE OSTIENSE

VIA C. COLOMBO

VIA SOLARIA